About the book

This book is compilation of my select digital art works made before October 2016. Unlike some of my mixed media works which can be categorized under process art that at times are completed over years, digital works, sketches, and only few layered acrylics have served as a close companion to translate my ideas into reality in a limited time. This book showcases different kinds of experiments, not necessarily the most pleasing or polished works. I made these works using mouse on my laptop with Adobe Photoshop software. Several of these works started out as blank sheet, while in few I took help of an initial photograph. I have occasionally clicked pictures of my oil, water, or acrylic paintings and digitally modified them to see how an altered rendition of the same painting would like, enabling a quick study before committing myself to canvas. This book brings to you a compilation of select works that depict my different uses of digital medium for still painting until 2016.

Contact Sukant Khurana at

https://twitter.com/sukant_khurana
http://www.brainnart.com

Photocredits: Costance Burkin Printed by Create Space 2016

Inspired by music

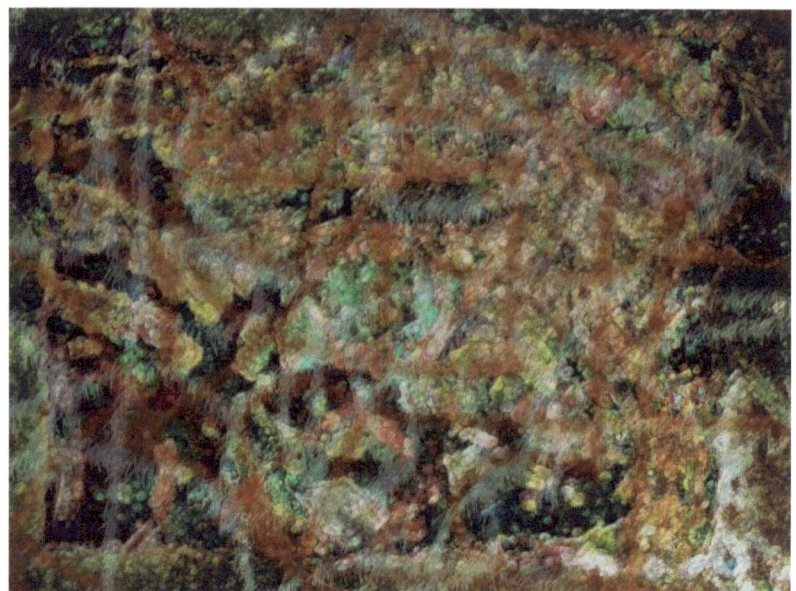

Pleasant sounds...

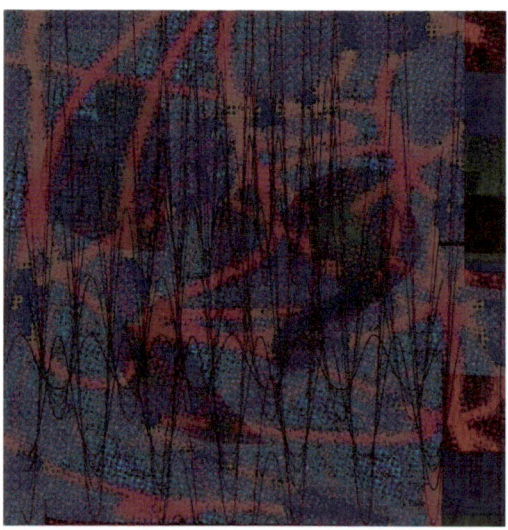

Instant noodles with a lots of love. It doesn't matter if I am saying anything, I know what you hear is a melody!

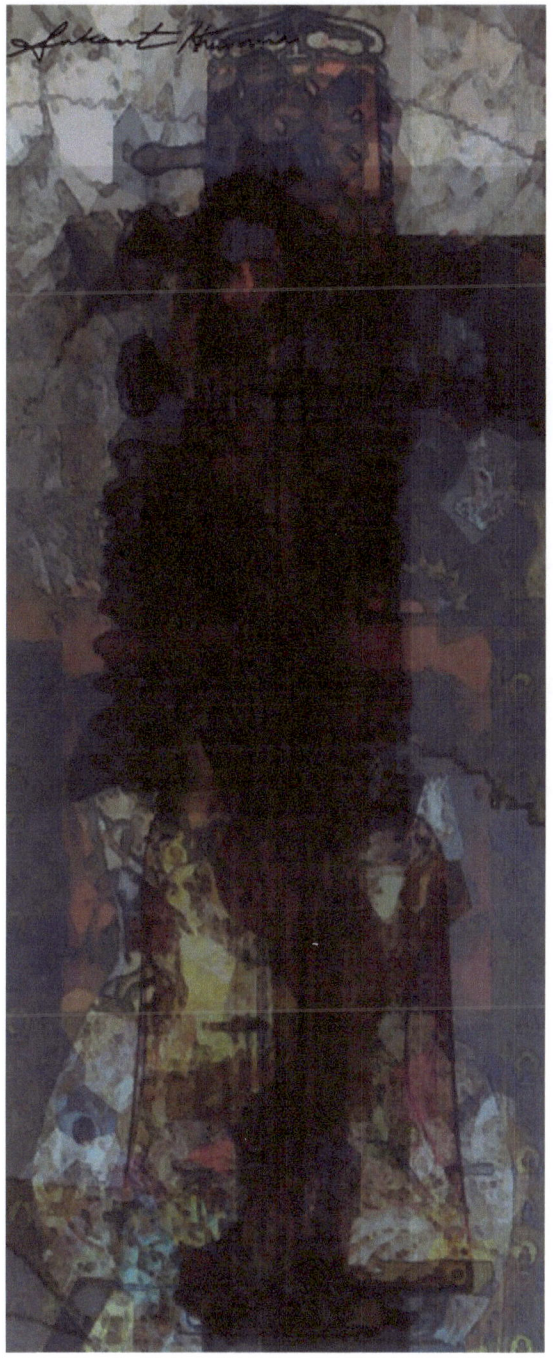

Sarangi, a musical instrument from South Asia

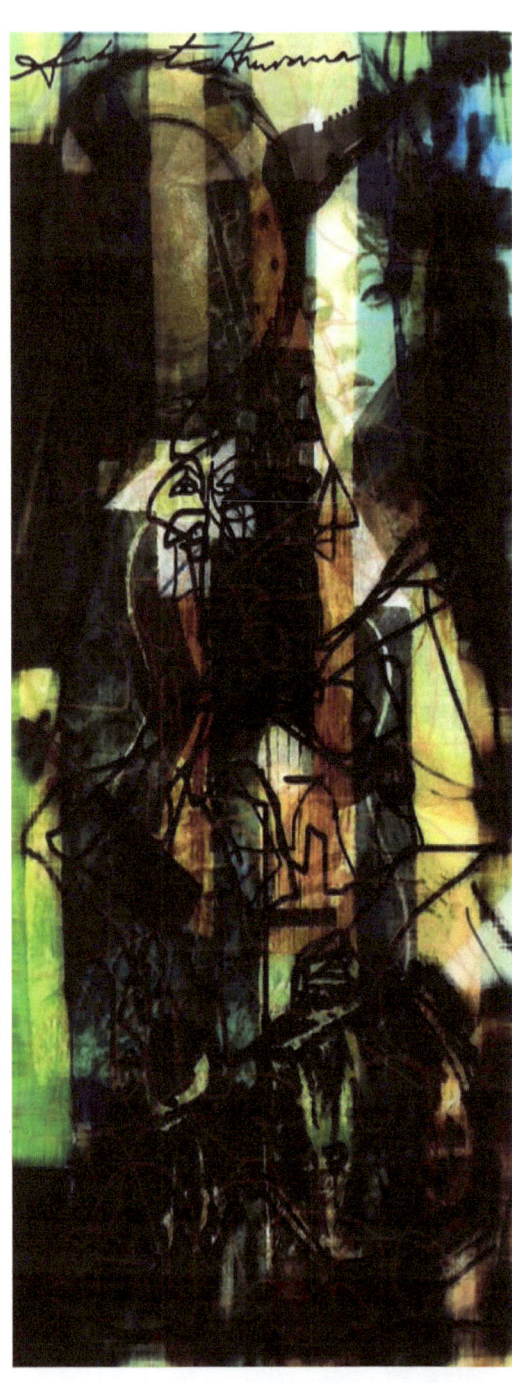

Jazz, with
instruments
from Asia

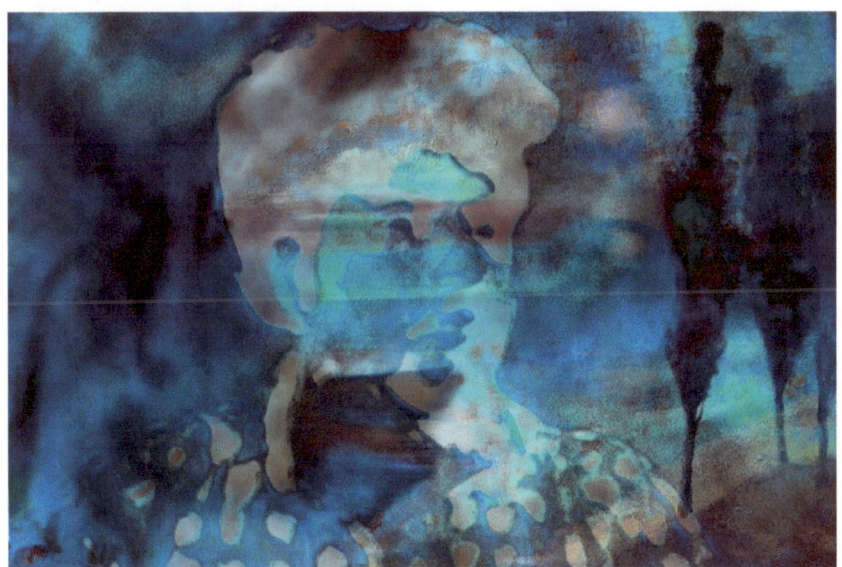

Self portrait of being immersed in blues.

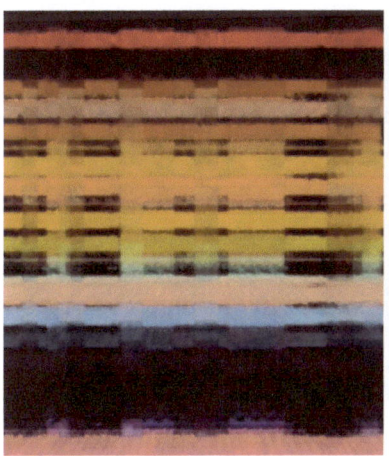

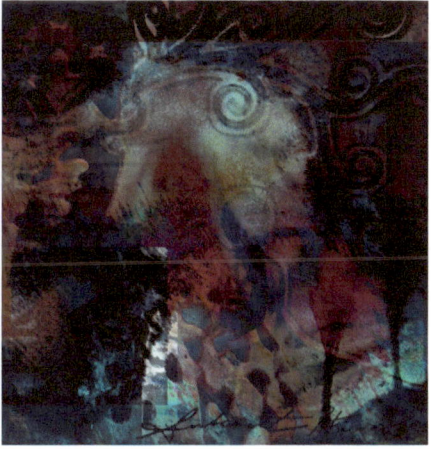

Rhythm on radio on drive
back home on a long evening

Pleasure in expressionistic music
landscape

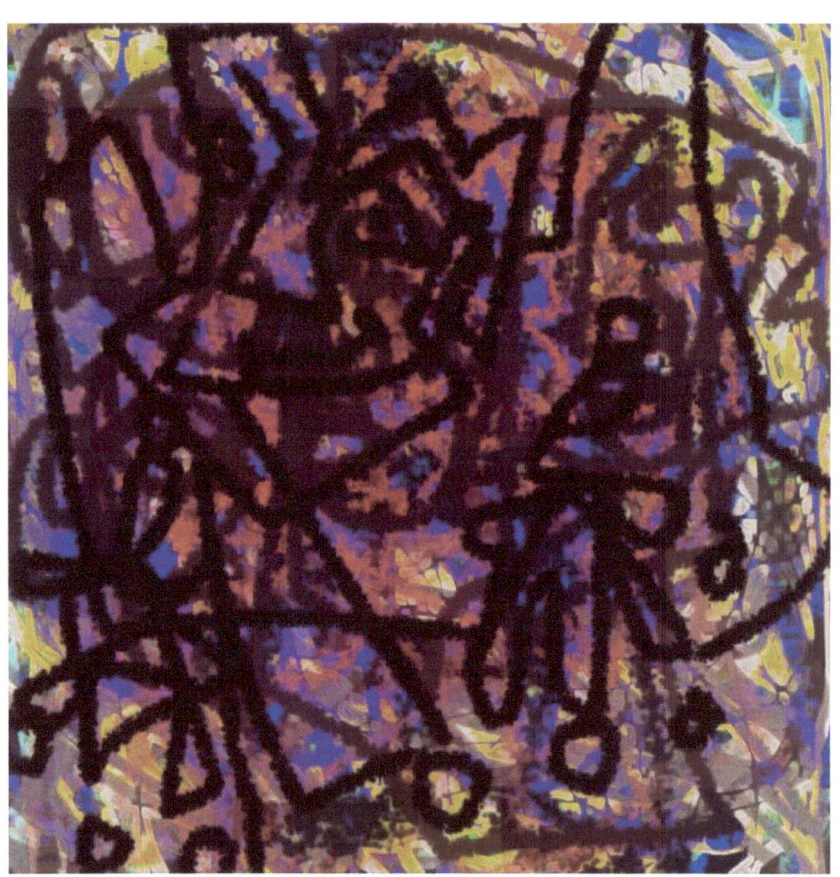

Pattern within patterns

What's wrong with love?

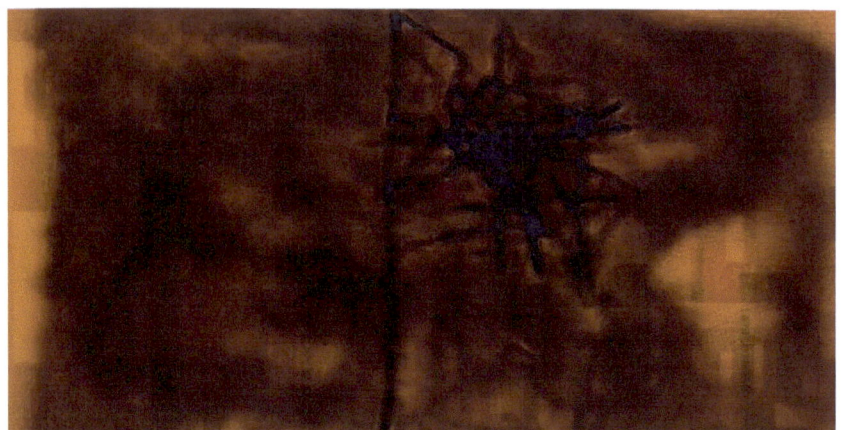

The promised tryst

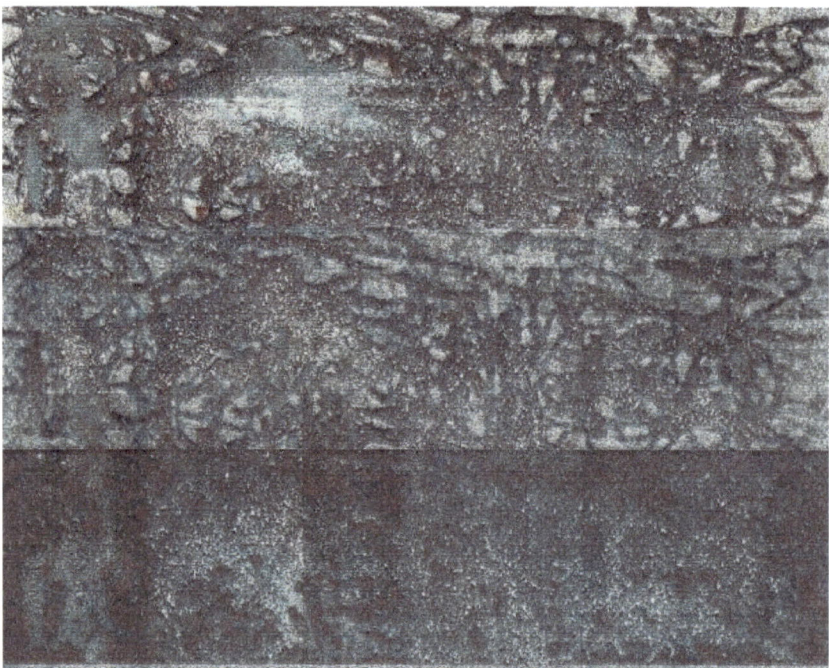

As if we never met (same pattern as used in "Deconstruction of love"; a play of contours)

Deconstruction of love – 3 works on play of colors to express different feelings.

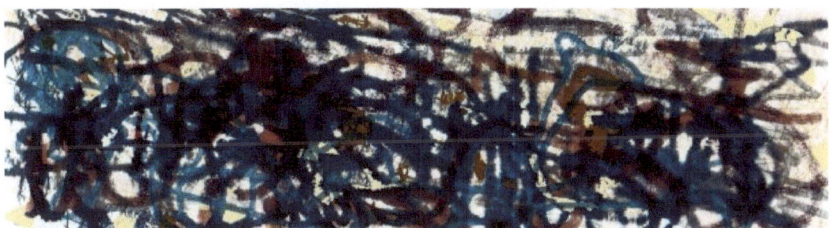

Deconstruction of love: the first time.

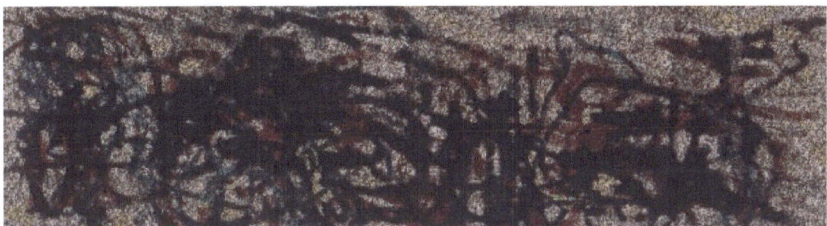

Deconstruction of love: remembering the two week high.

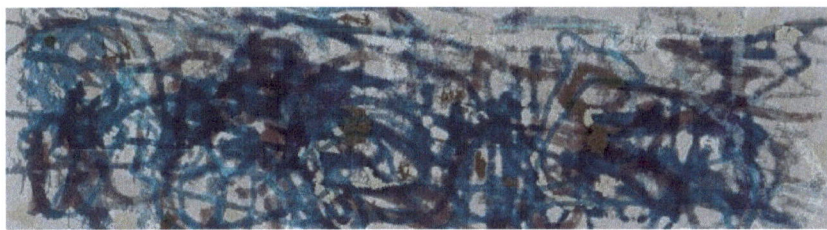

Deconstruction of love: remembering for the sake of remembering.

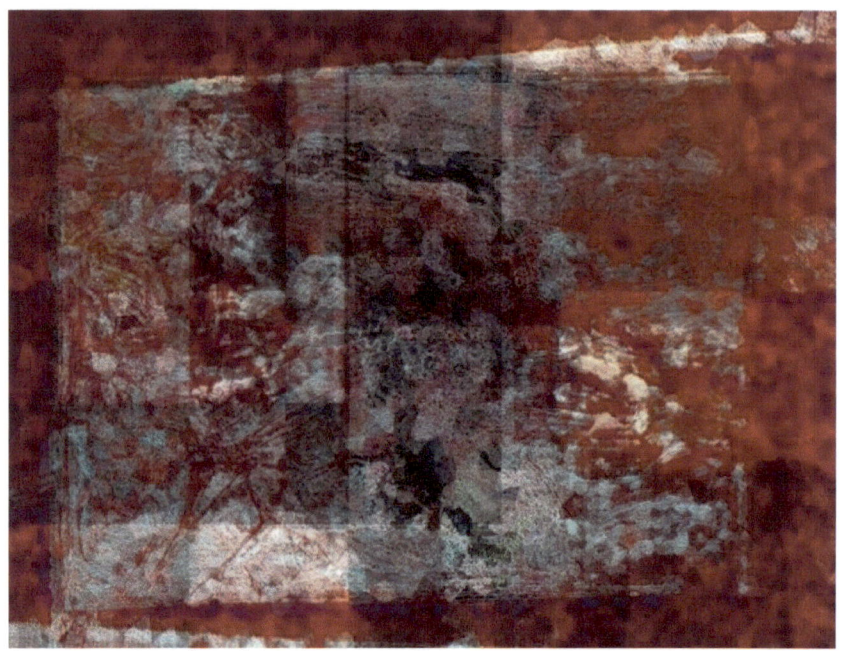

Deconstruction of an obsession.

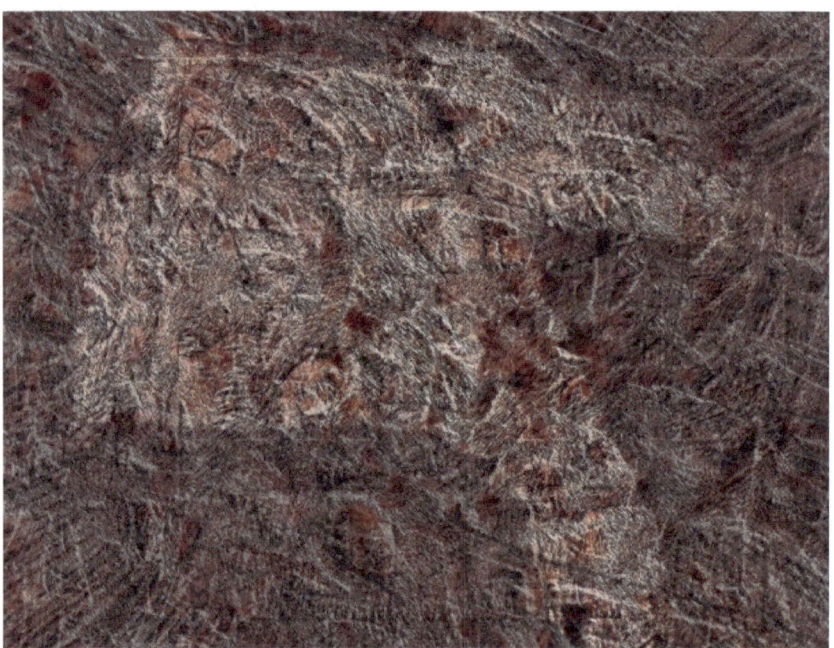

Deconstructing joy.

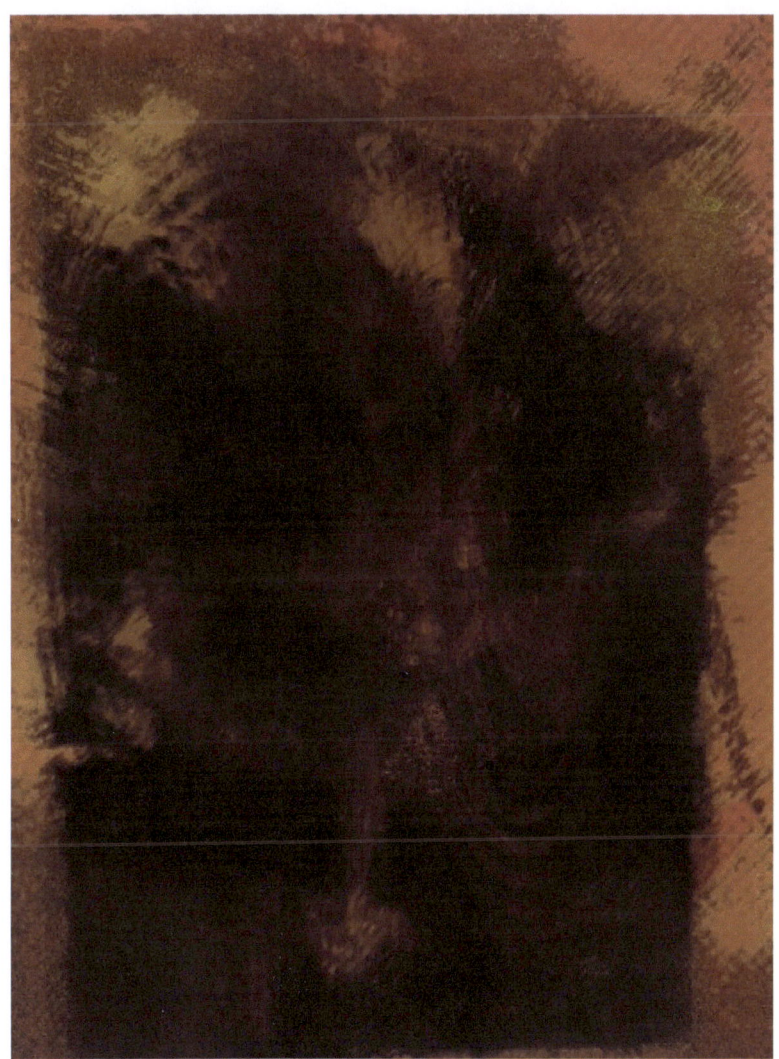

Anatomy of bonding.

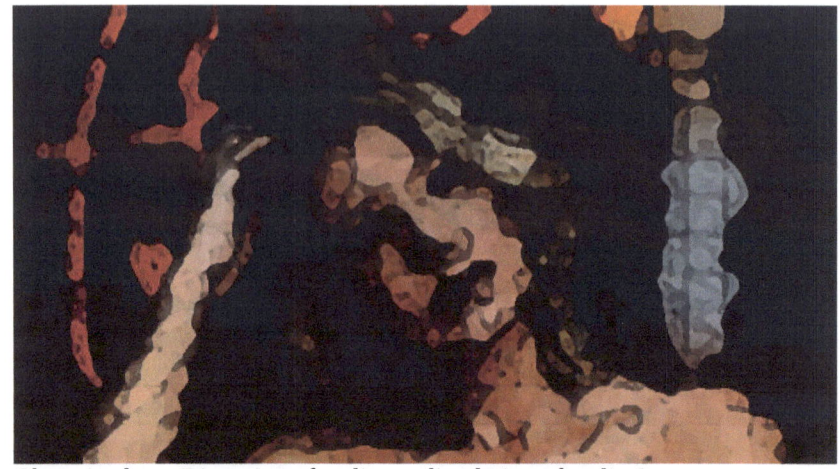
Obsessive love: Distortion of reality or dissolution of reality?

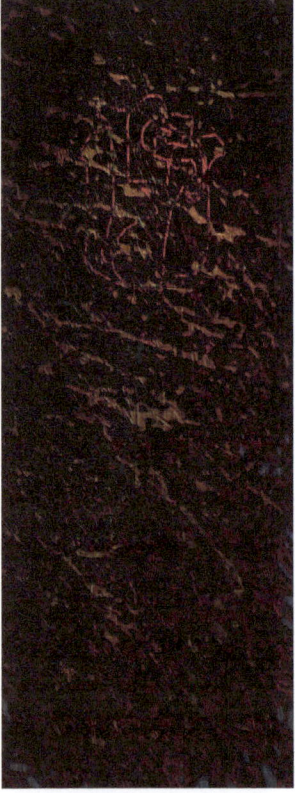

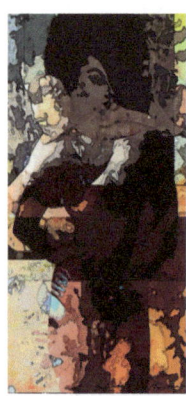
Juxtaposition of some famous nudes with coloring changed to the way I like it.

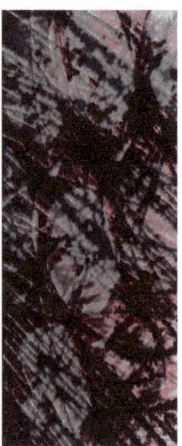
Reconstructing another obsession: puzzled after inability to find anything beyond myself.

Remembering and regretting not saying something stupid.

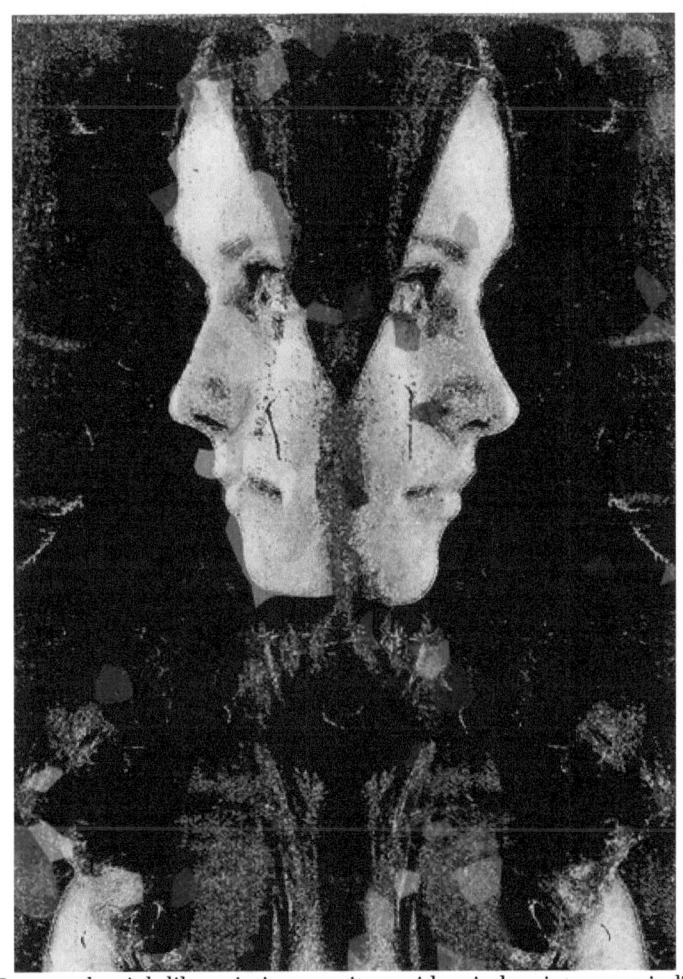

Just another ink-like painting; can it provide window into my mind?

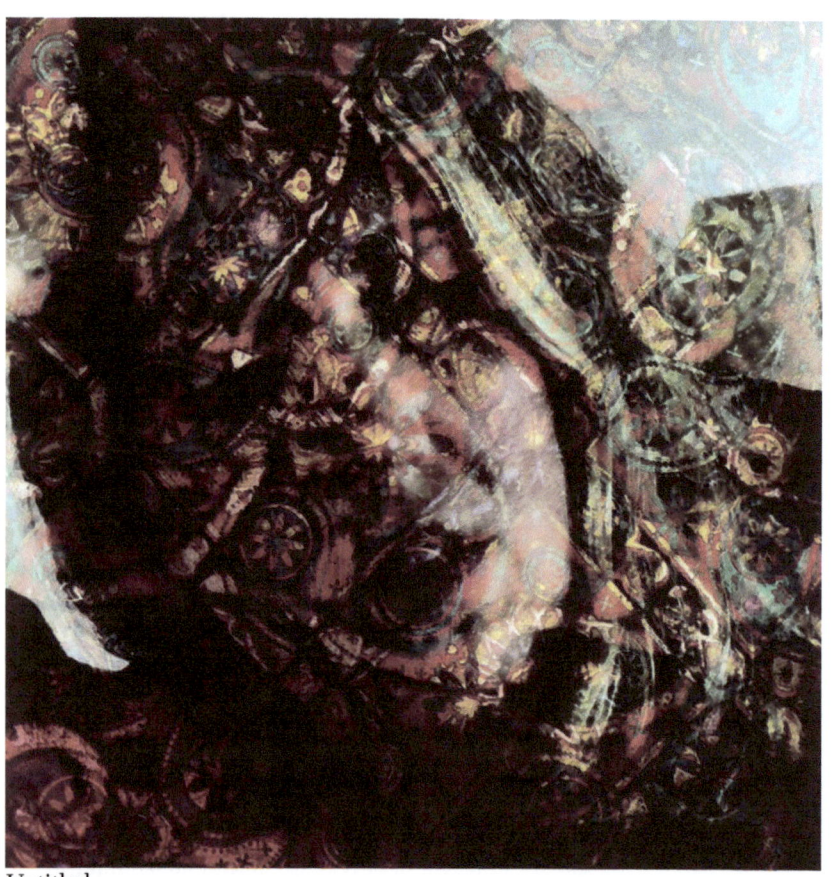

Untitled

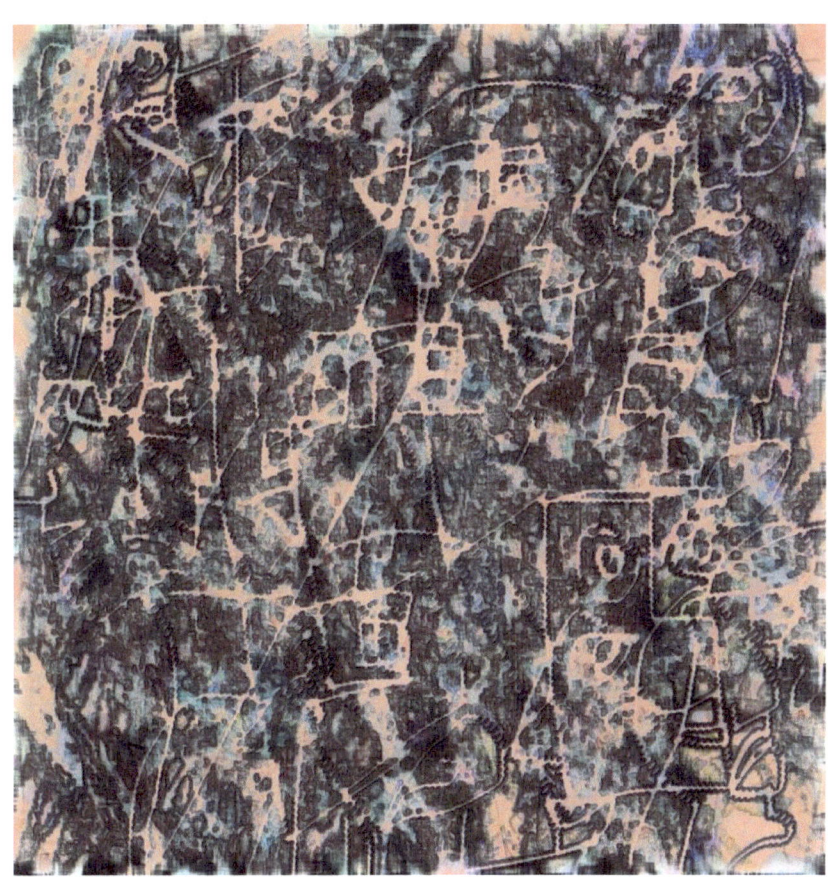

You can wail here if you wish!

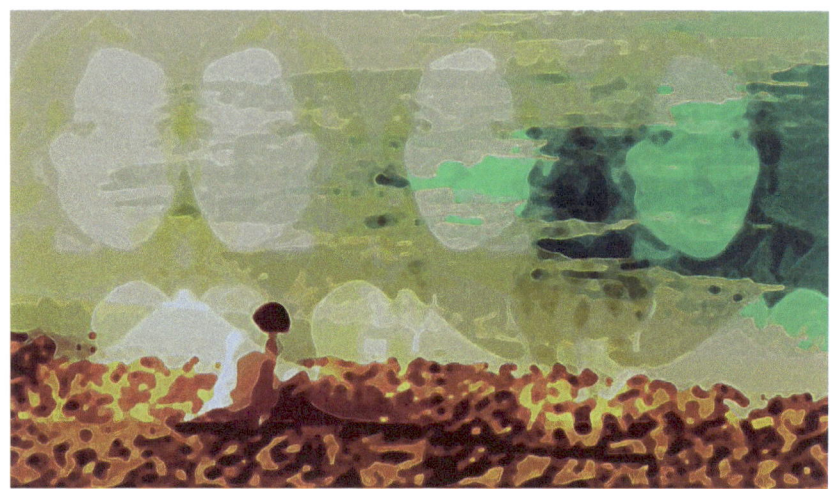

A meeting at the harbor

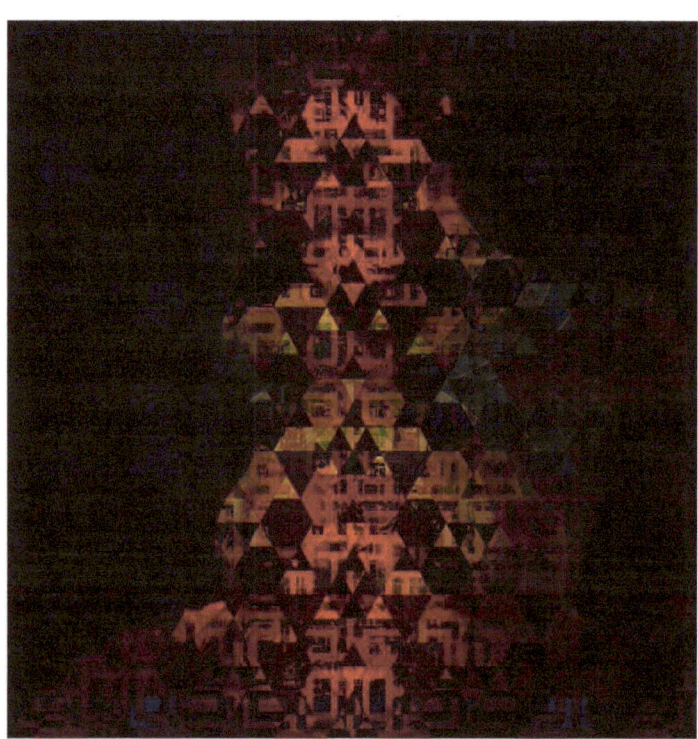

Ah...the excitement of symmetry!

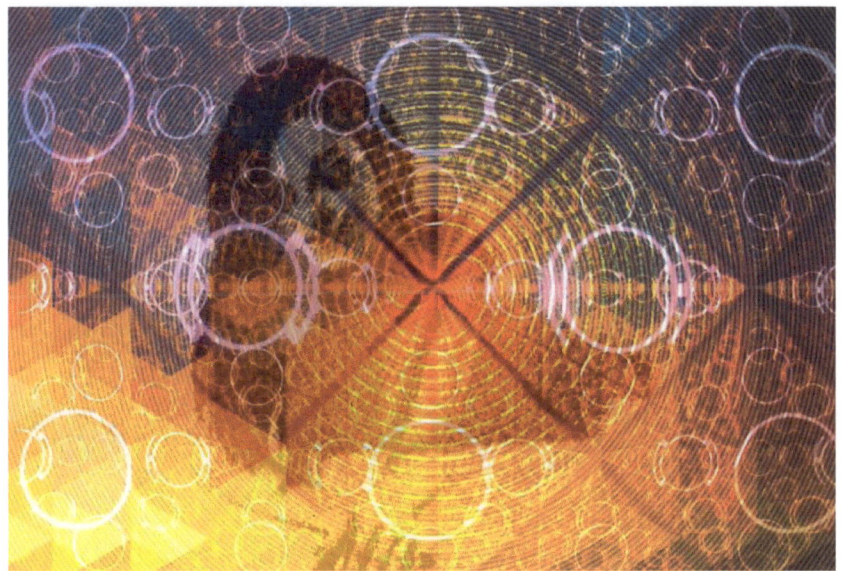

Play with geometry and some common threads

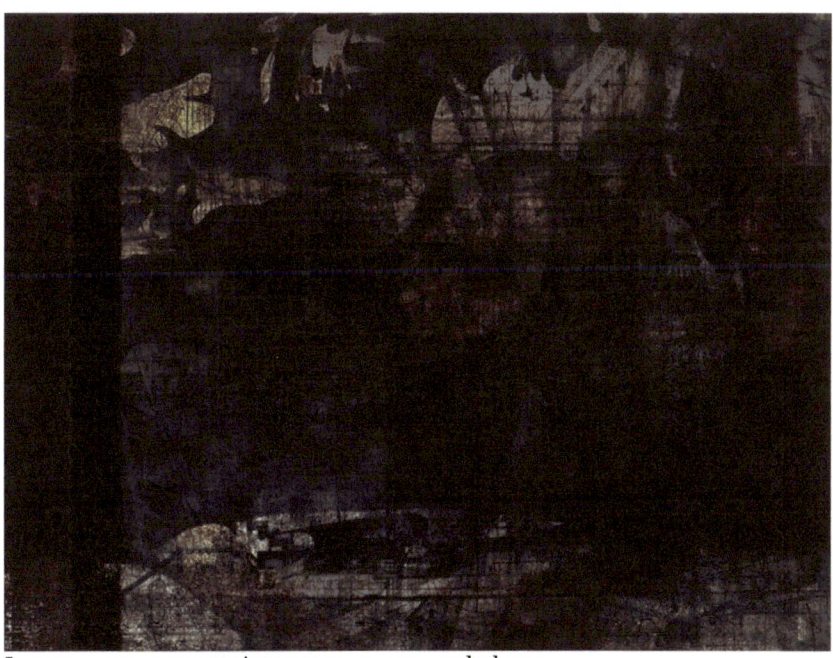

I am meet your memories at very unexpected places

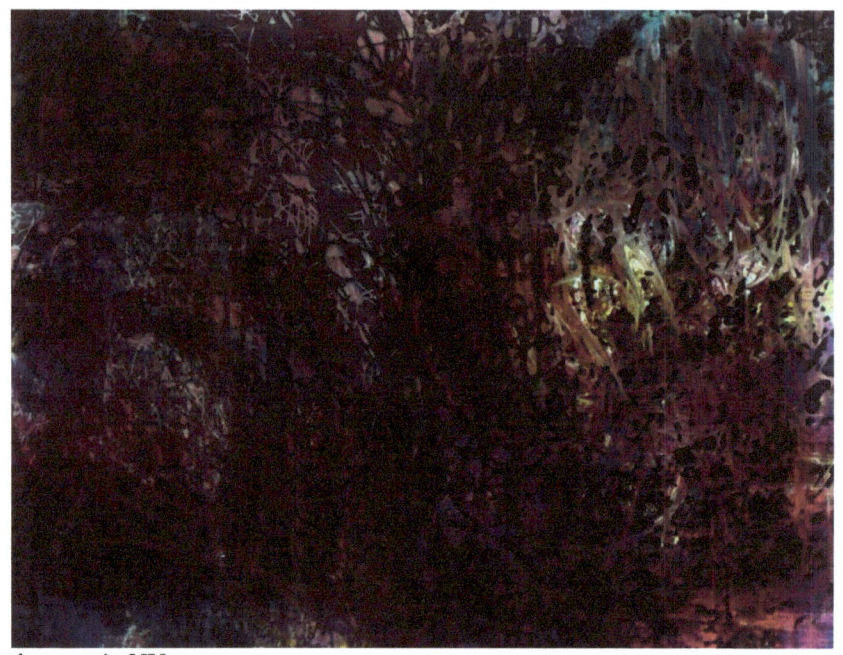

Autumn in NY

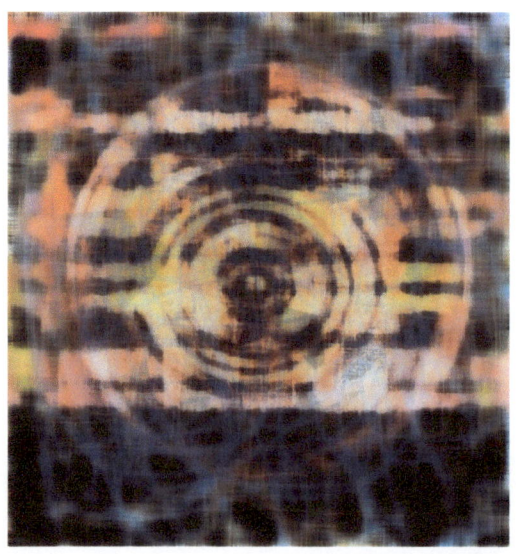

Memory of anger, without enthusiasm; almost peaceful.

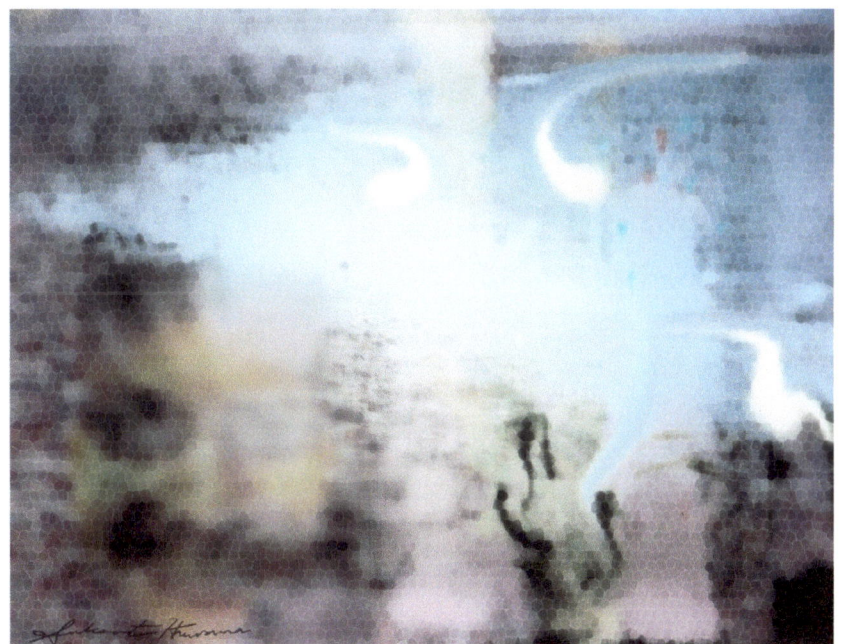

Delhi blues

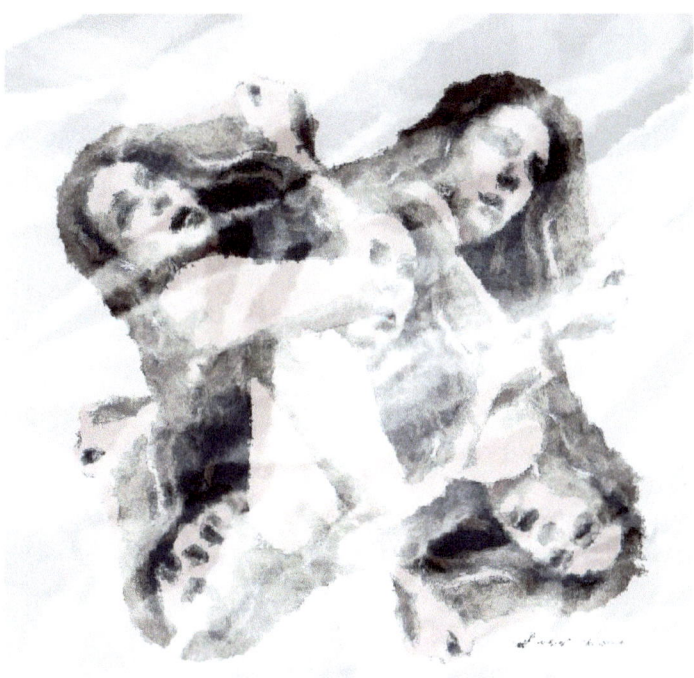

Circle of whatever

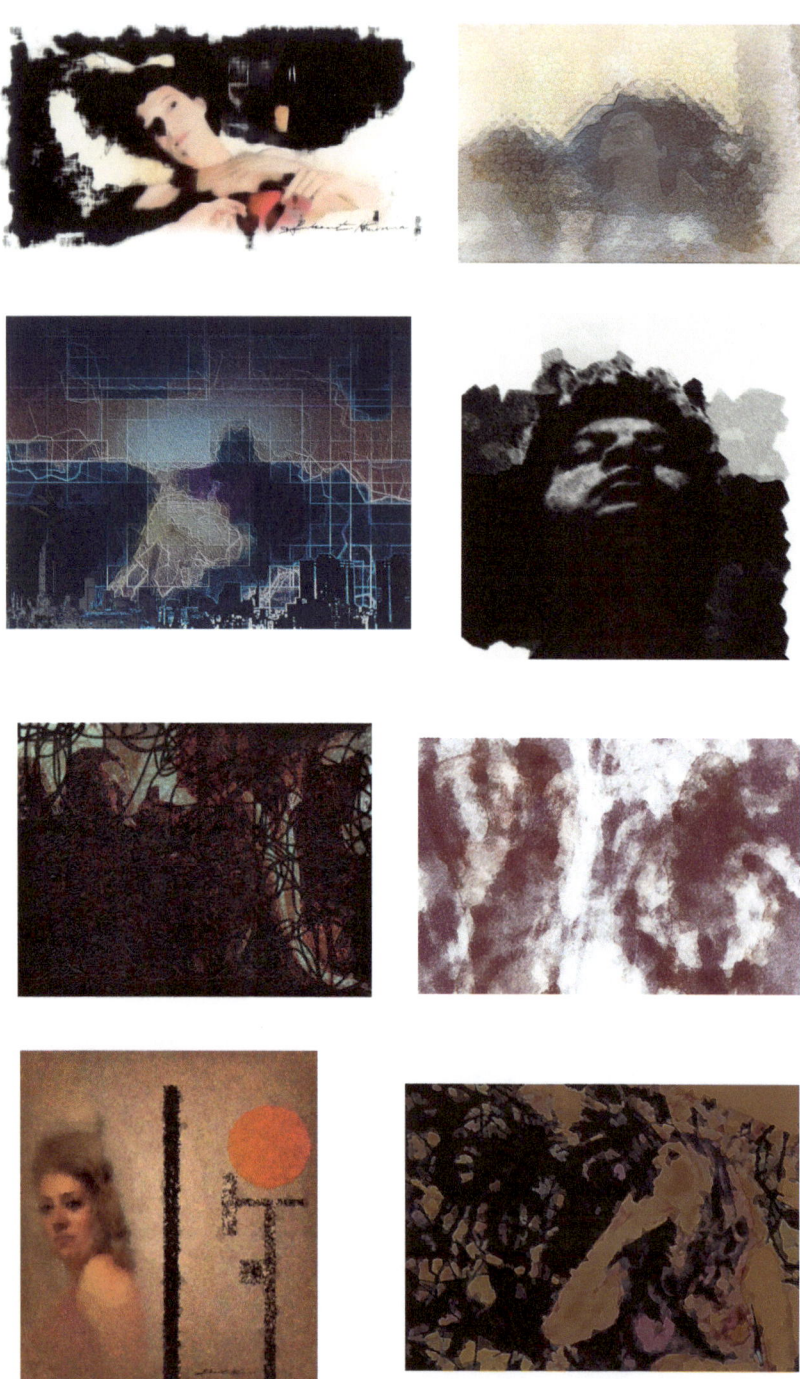

Case studies for other works, derived from photographs as starting point.

The year 2003

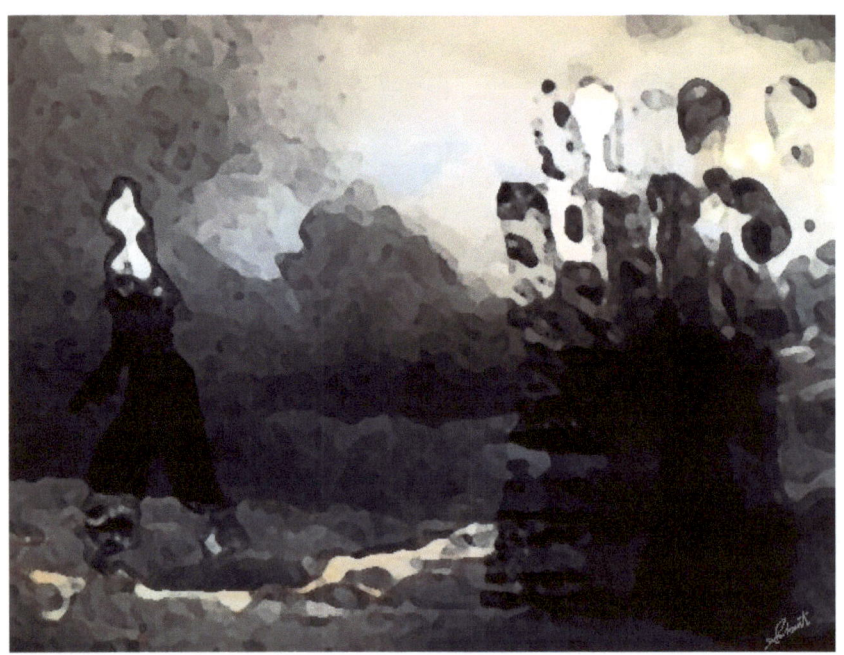
Moving away from oneself

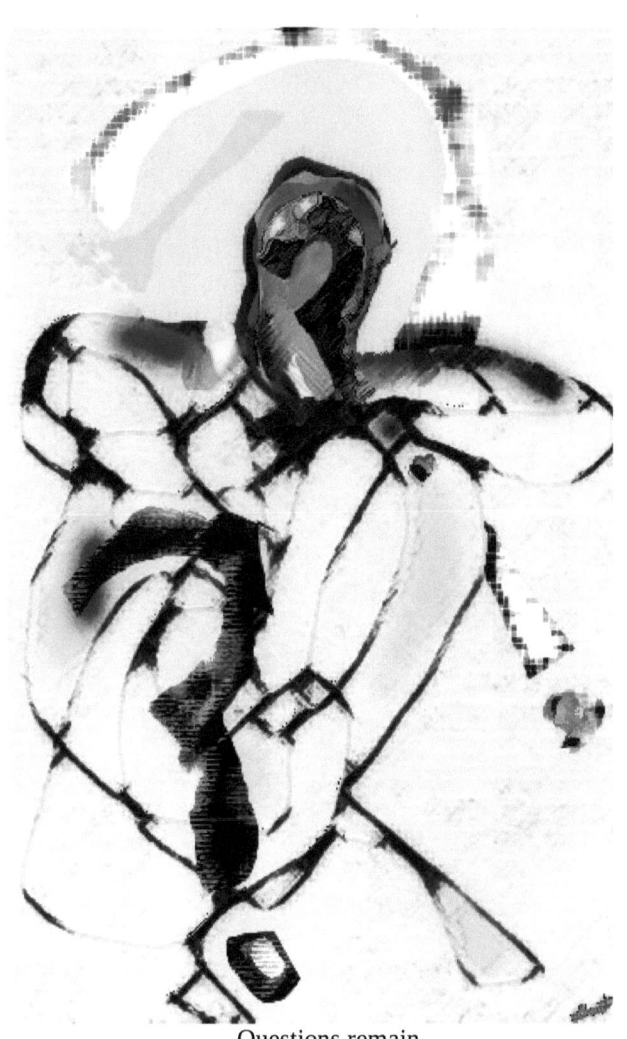

Questions remain

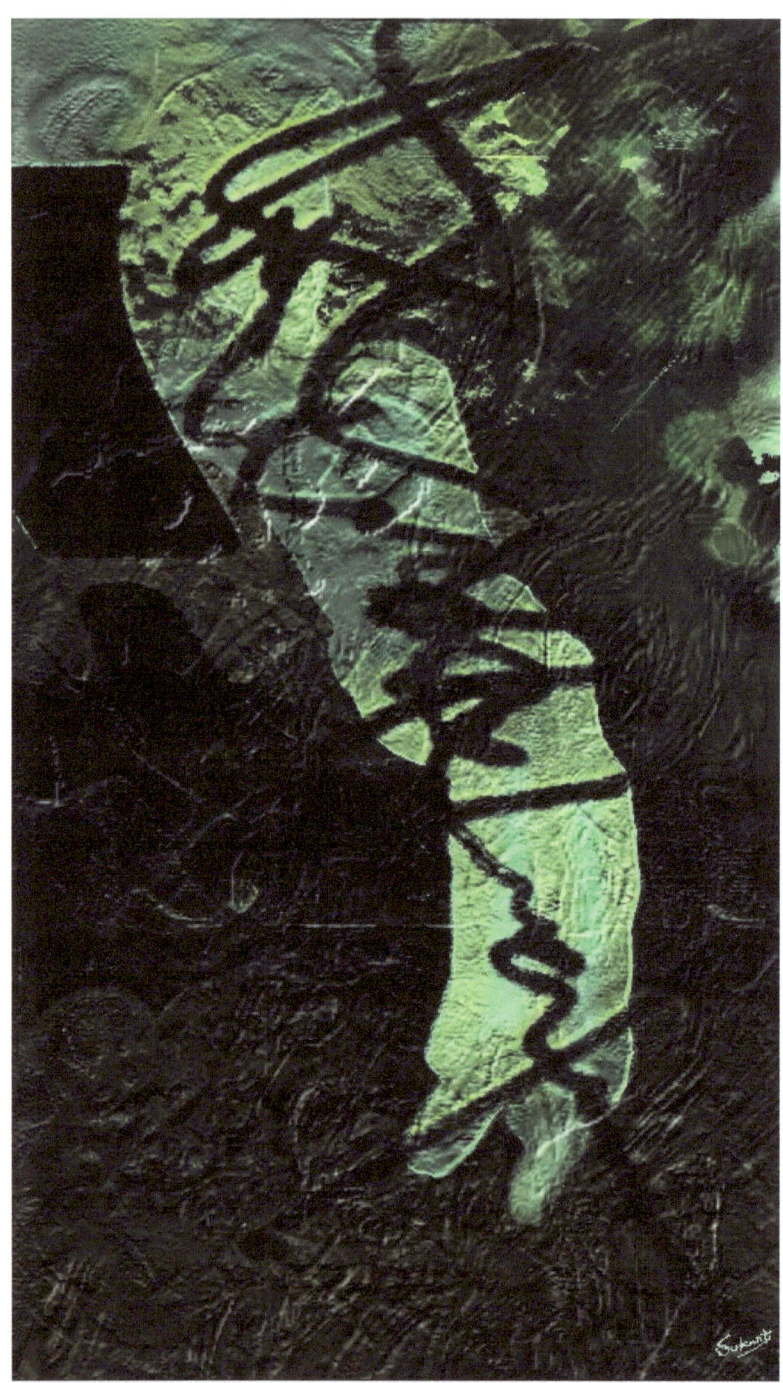

The green desert

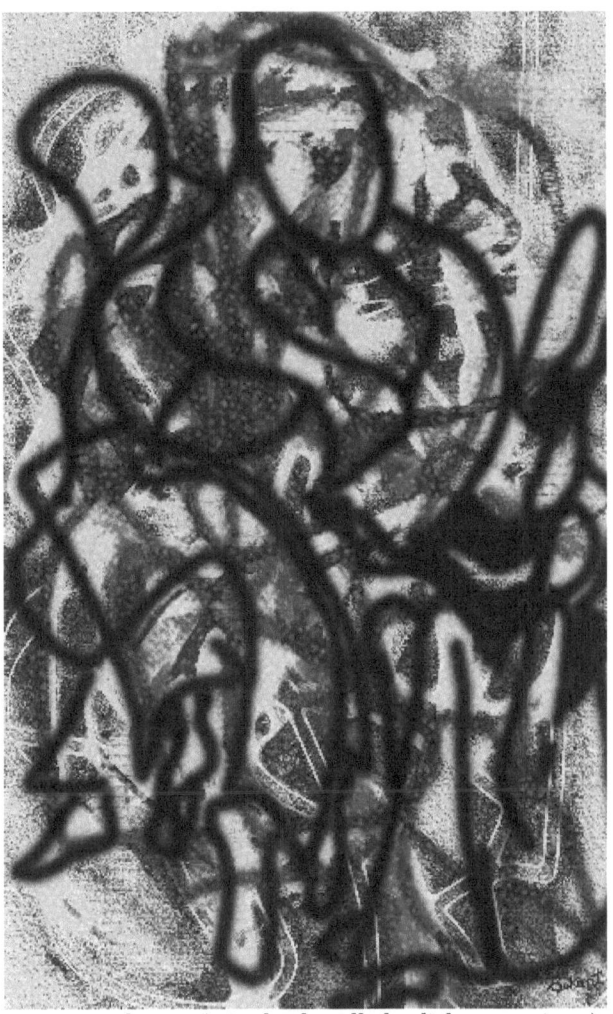
Two monologues (mistakenly called a dialogue at times)

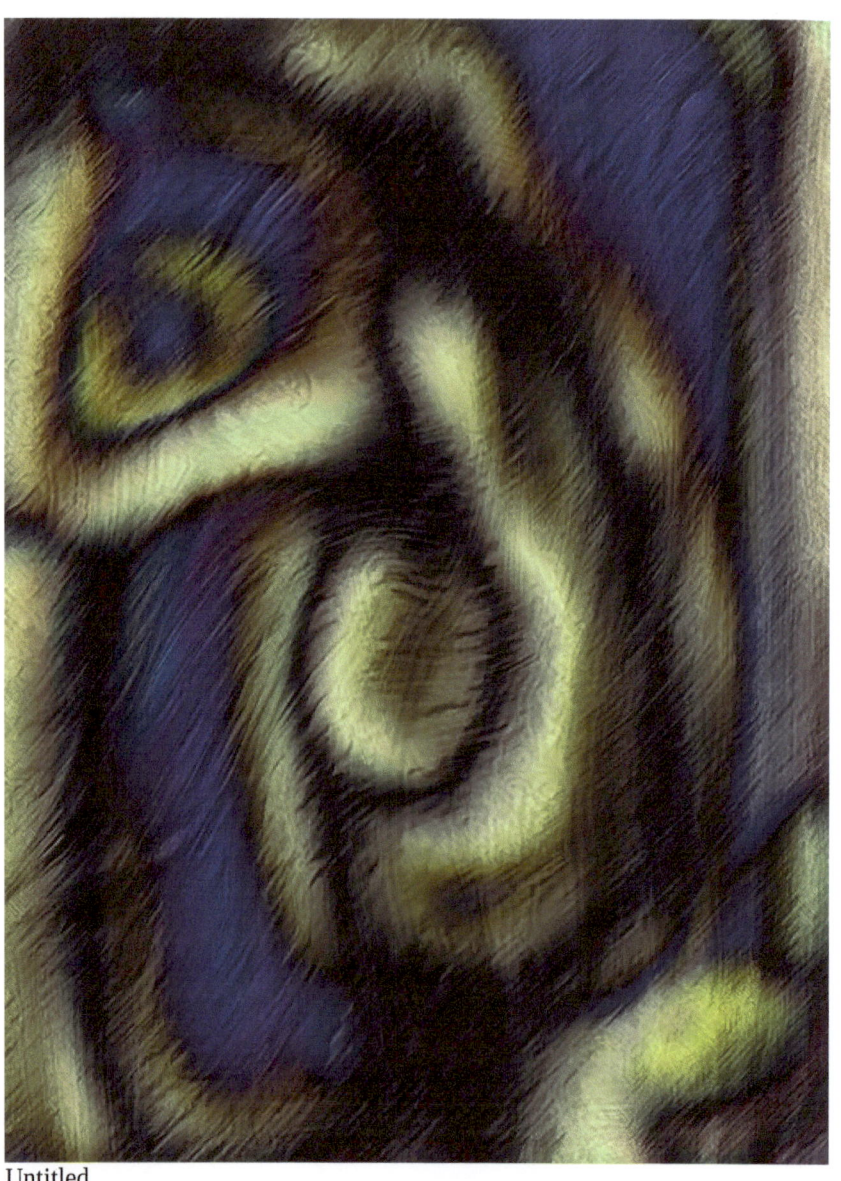

Untitled

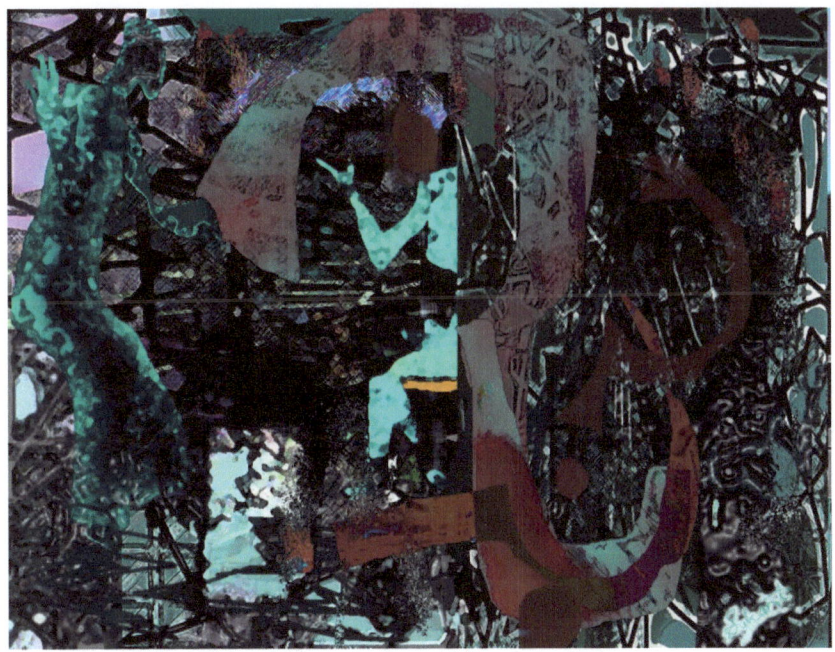

Life and revolution - in the middle of nowhere

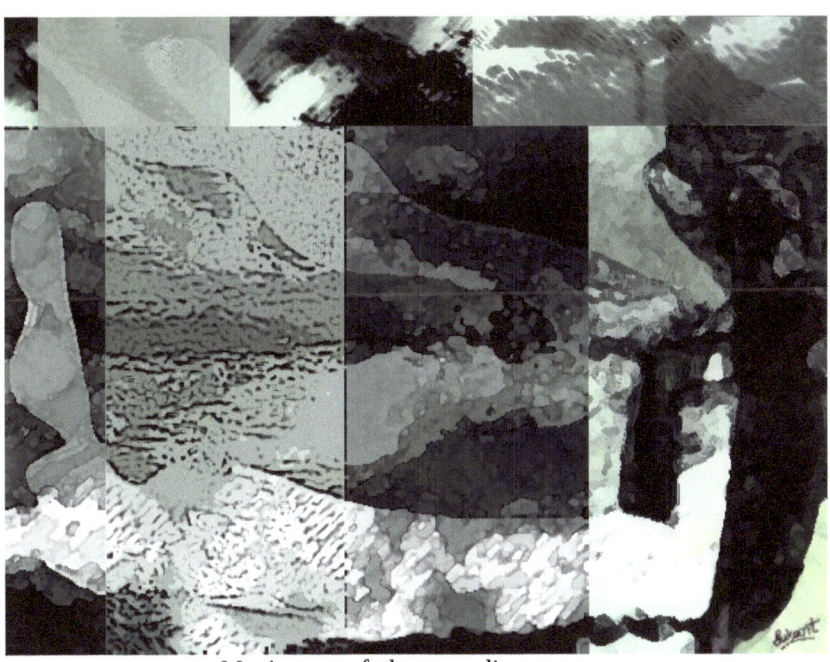

Moving out of glass paradise

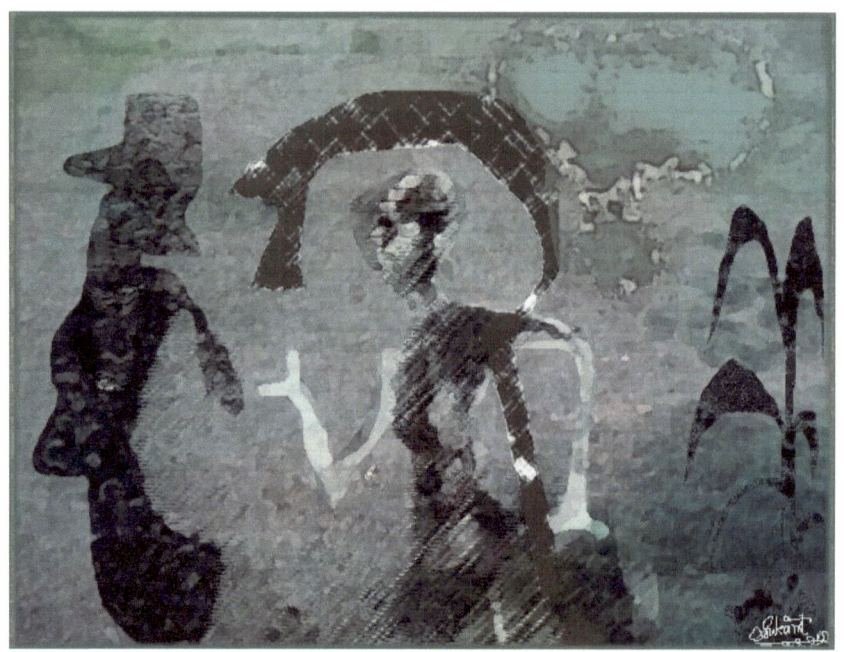

The ground reality

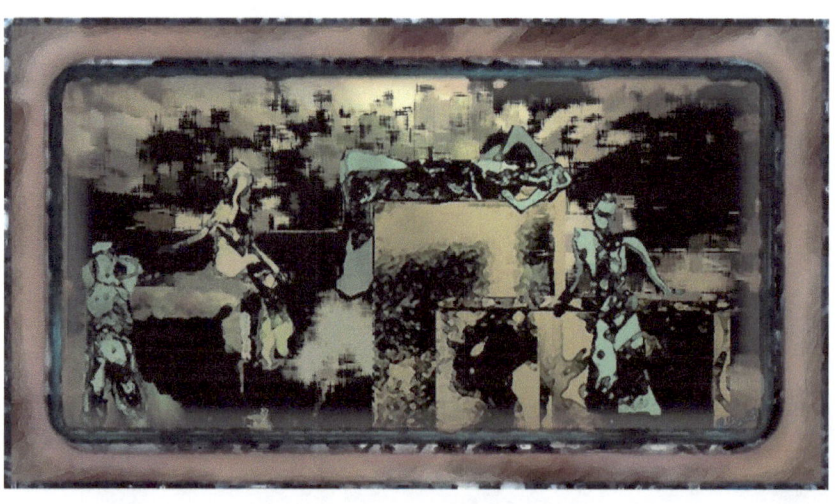

Remembering old days of college in Delhi, strolling streets of Bangalore

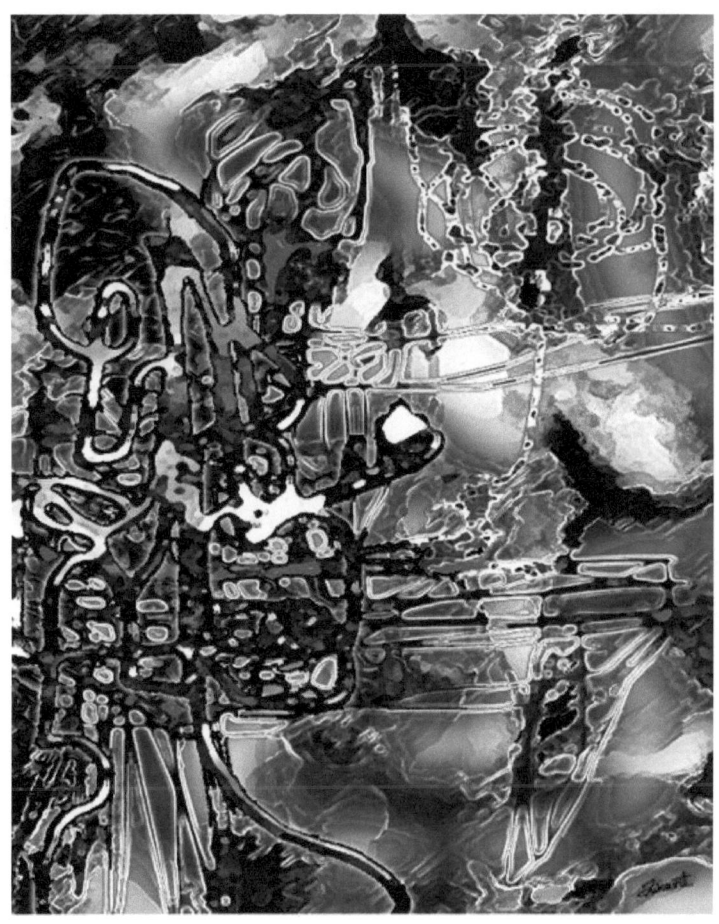

Dance of light patches on the wall

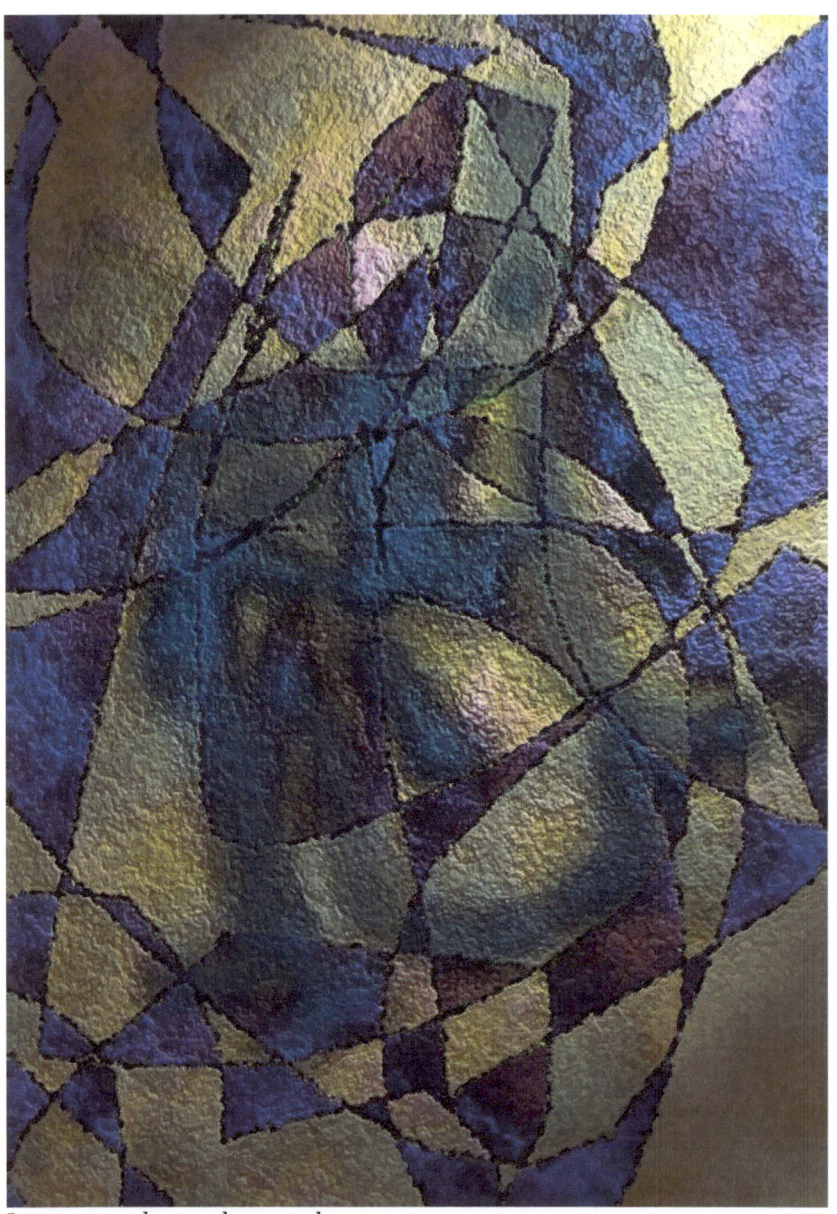

Leave me a place underground

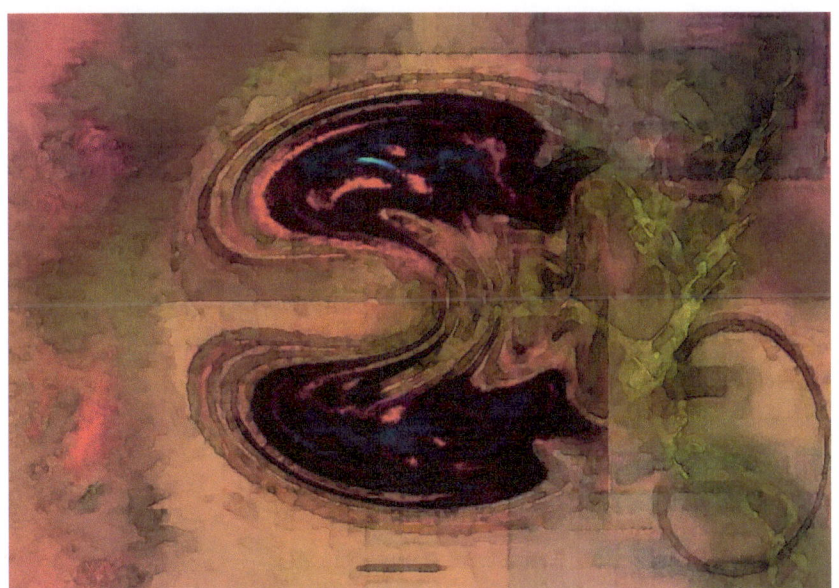

Exercise in narcism and conceit: Sukant atomicus

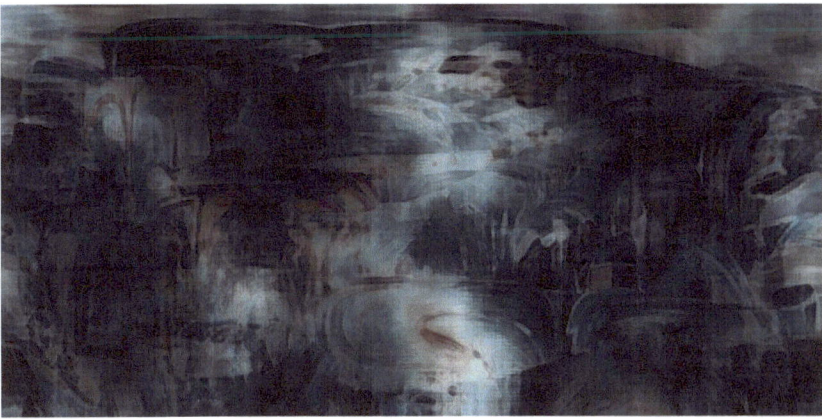

Untitled

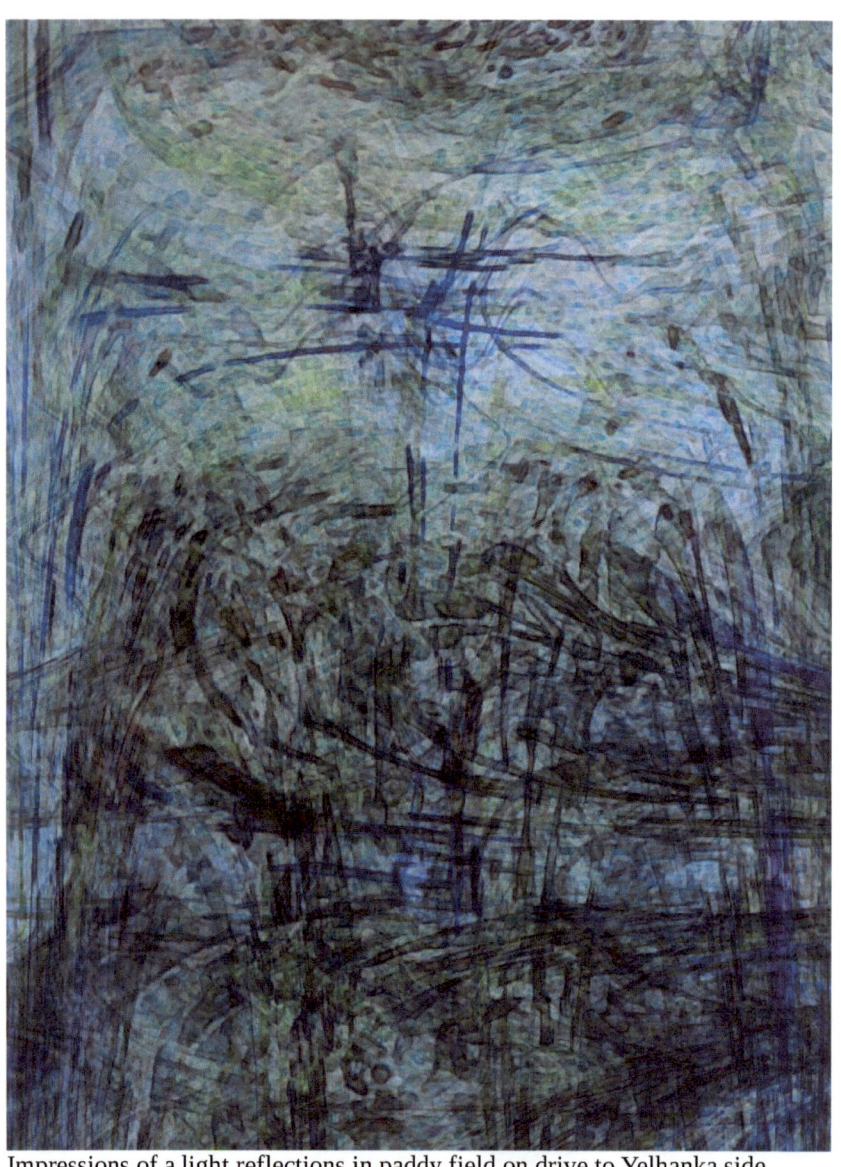

Impressions of a light reflections in paddy field on drive to Yelhanka side.

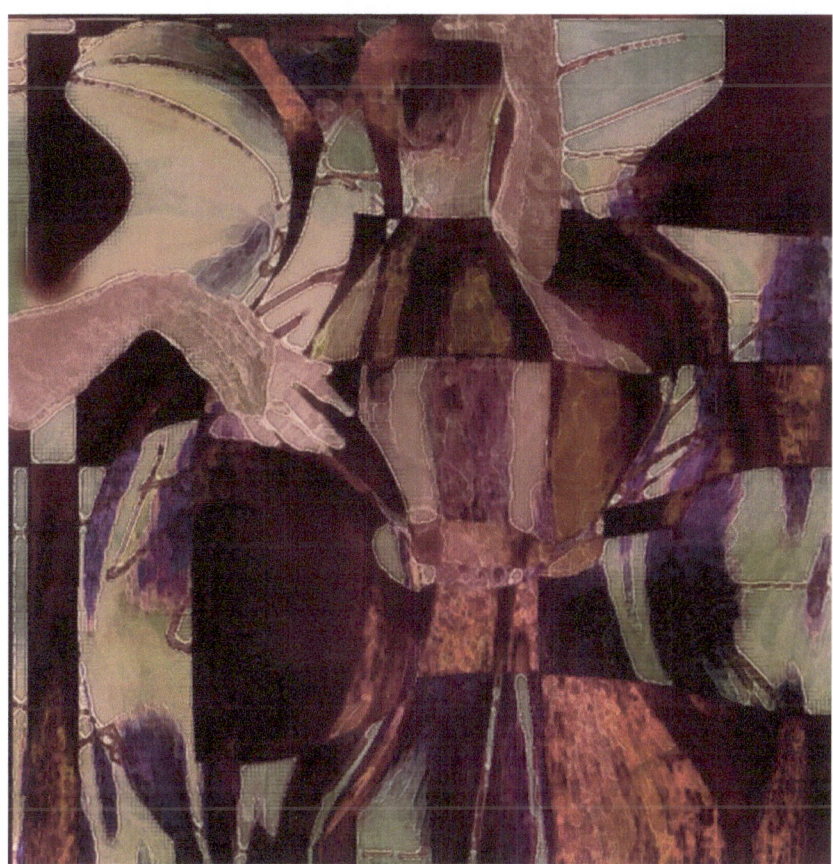

Holding the sky

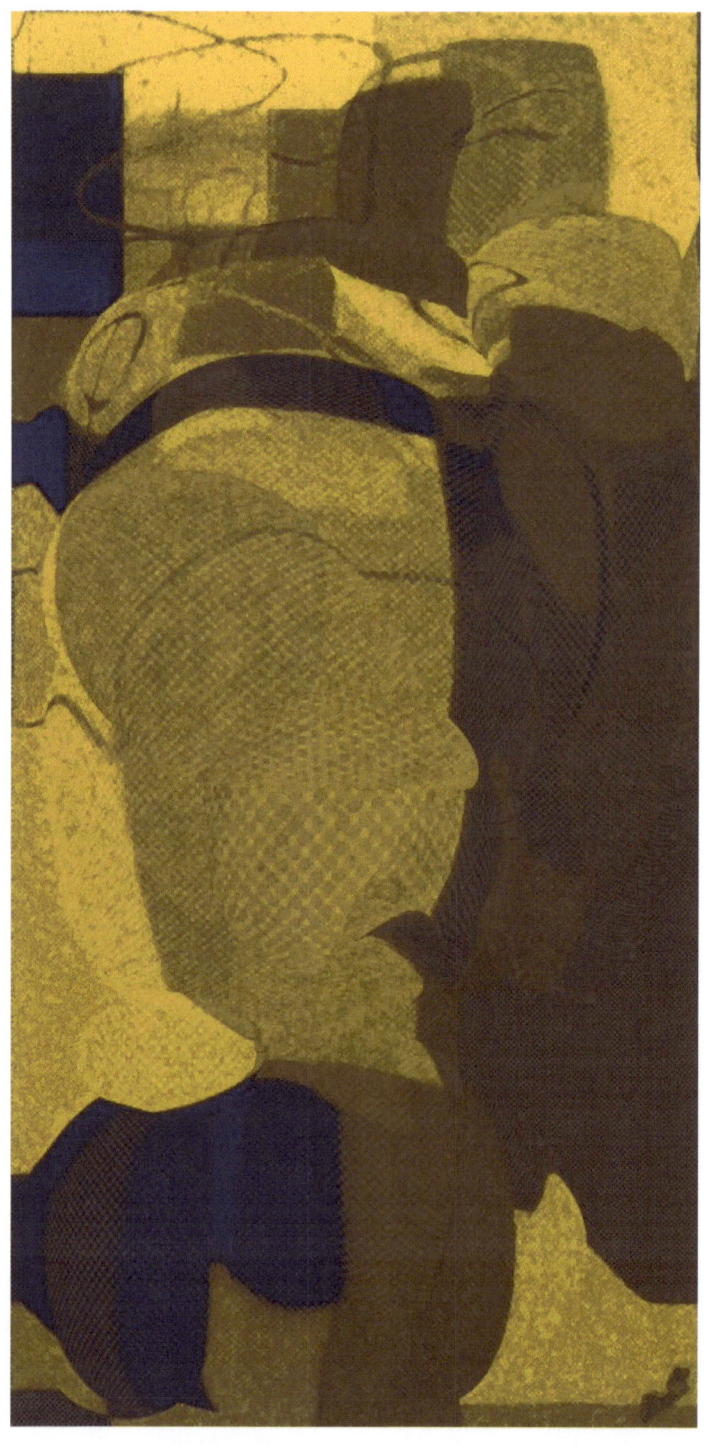

Listening
to some
nice jazz,
to take my
mind off
ongoing
problems

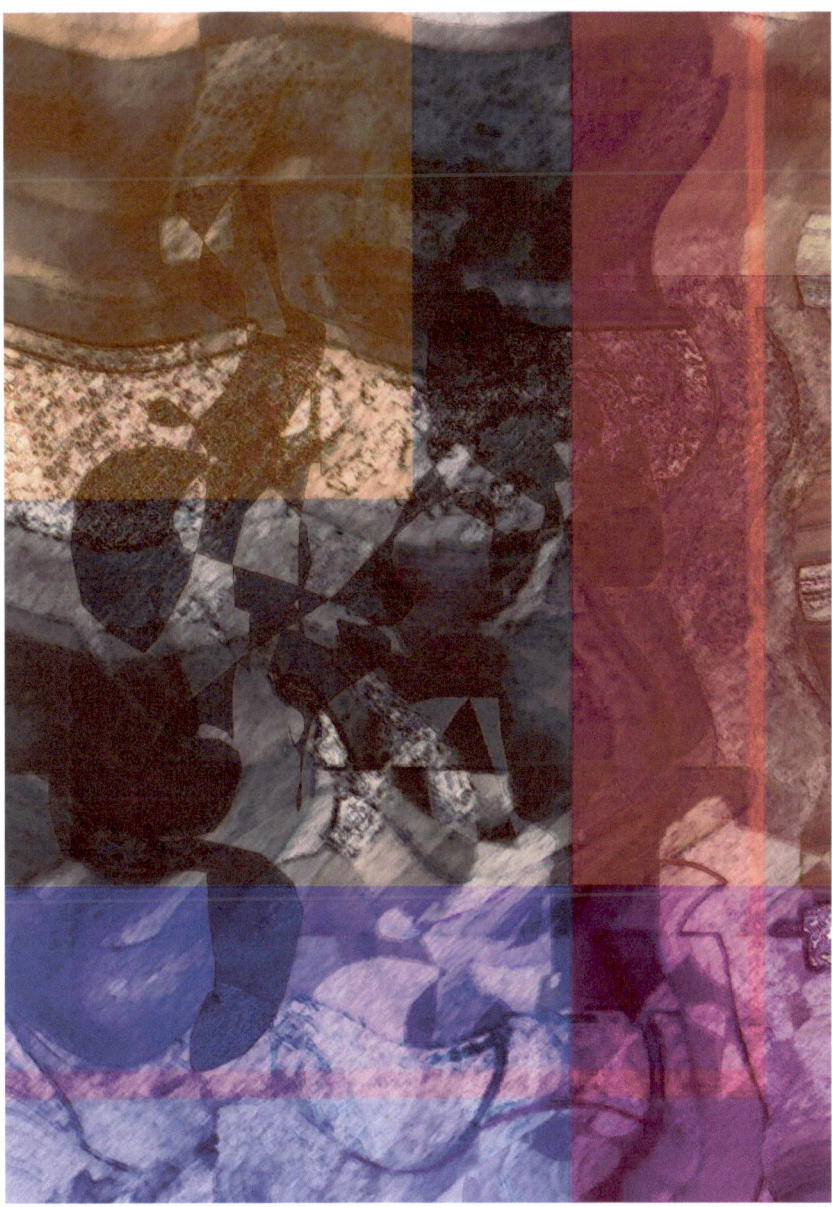

Untitled

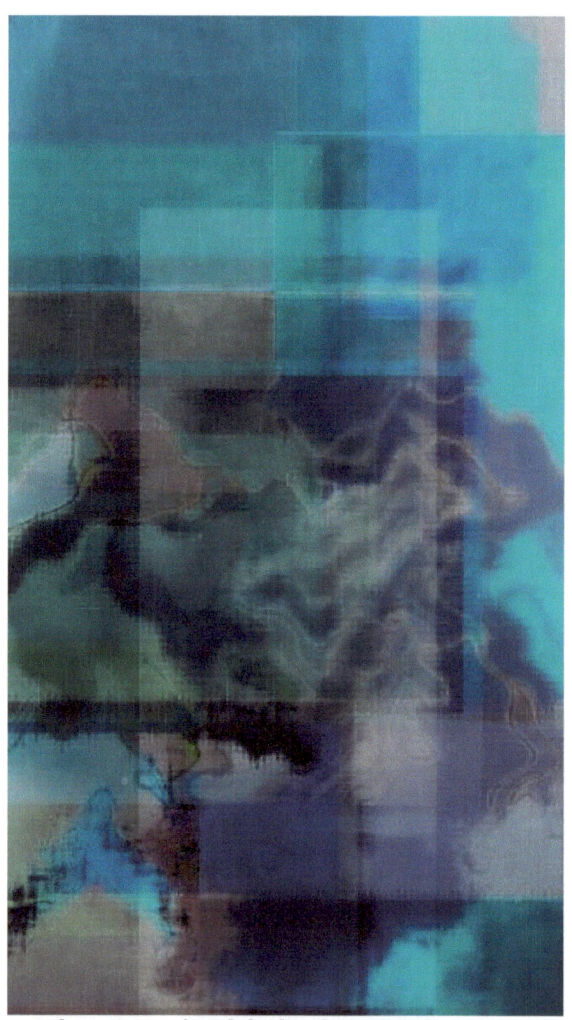

Where curves bend the harsh straight lines

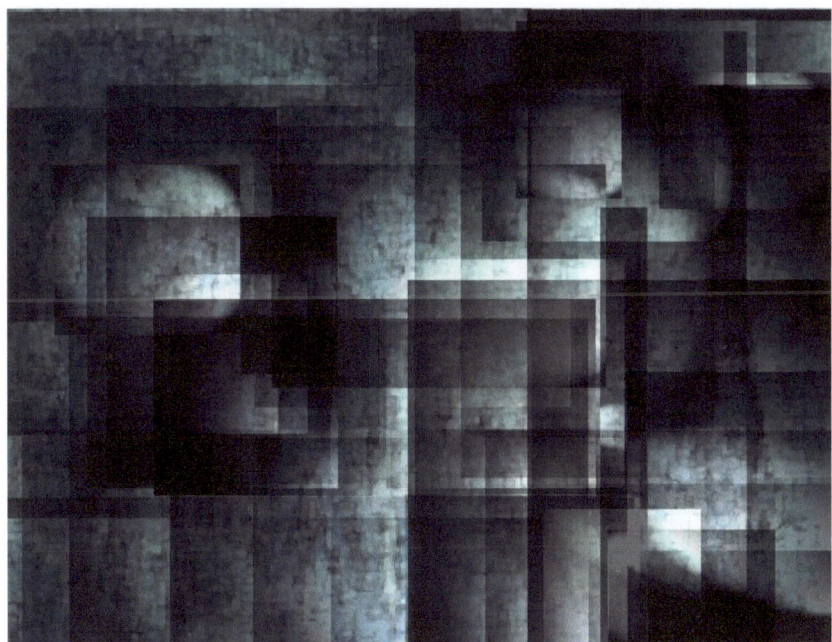

Some light finds its way through

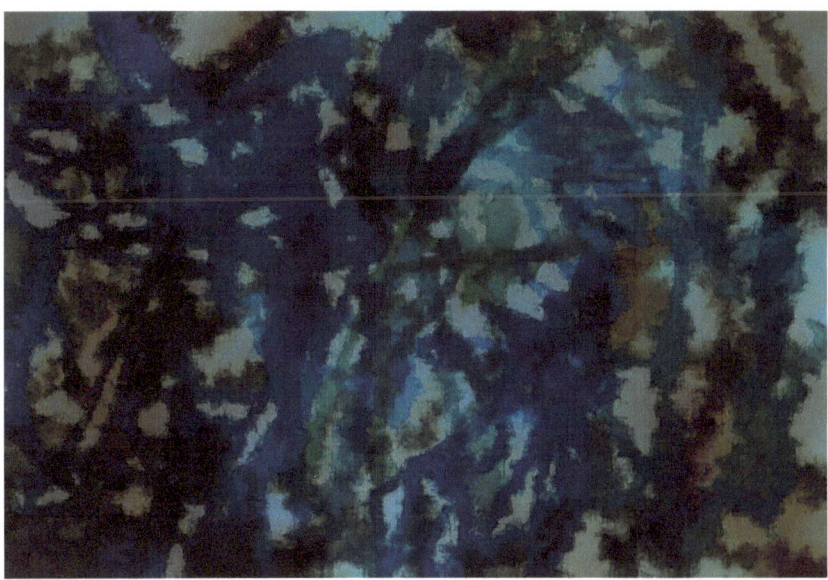

Dance of colors

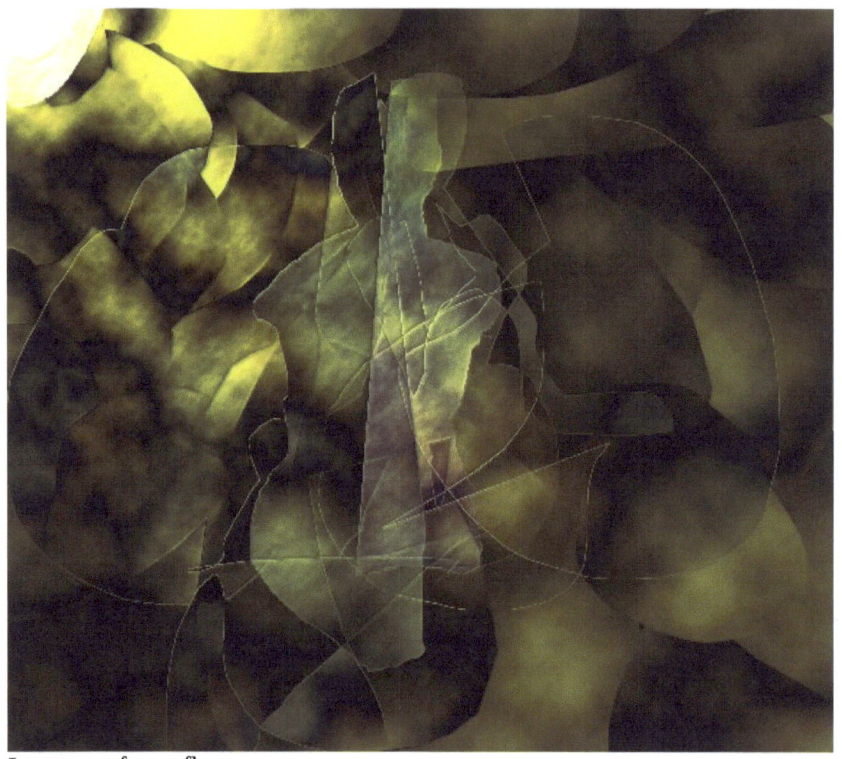

Leaves on forest floor

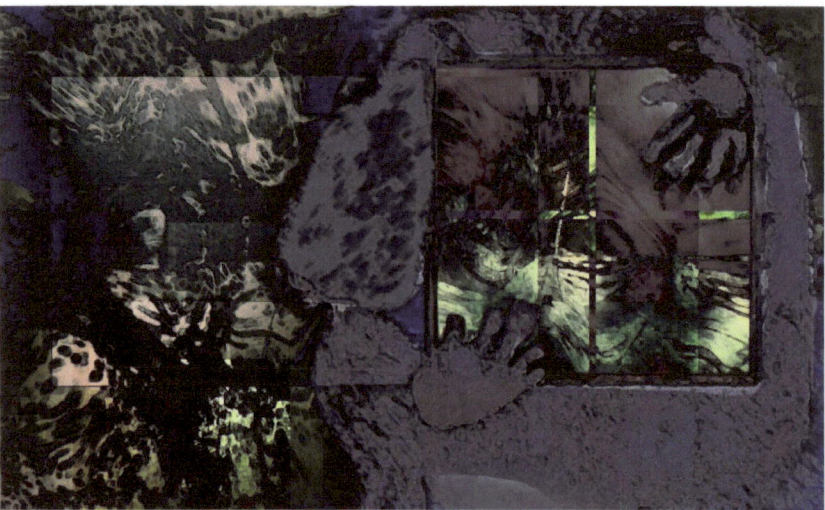

Window into the world

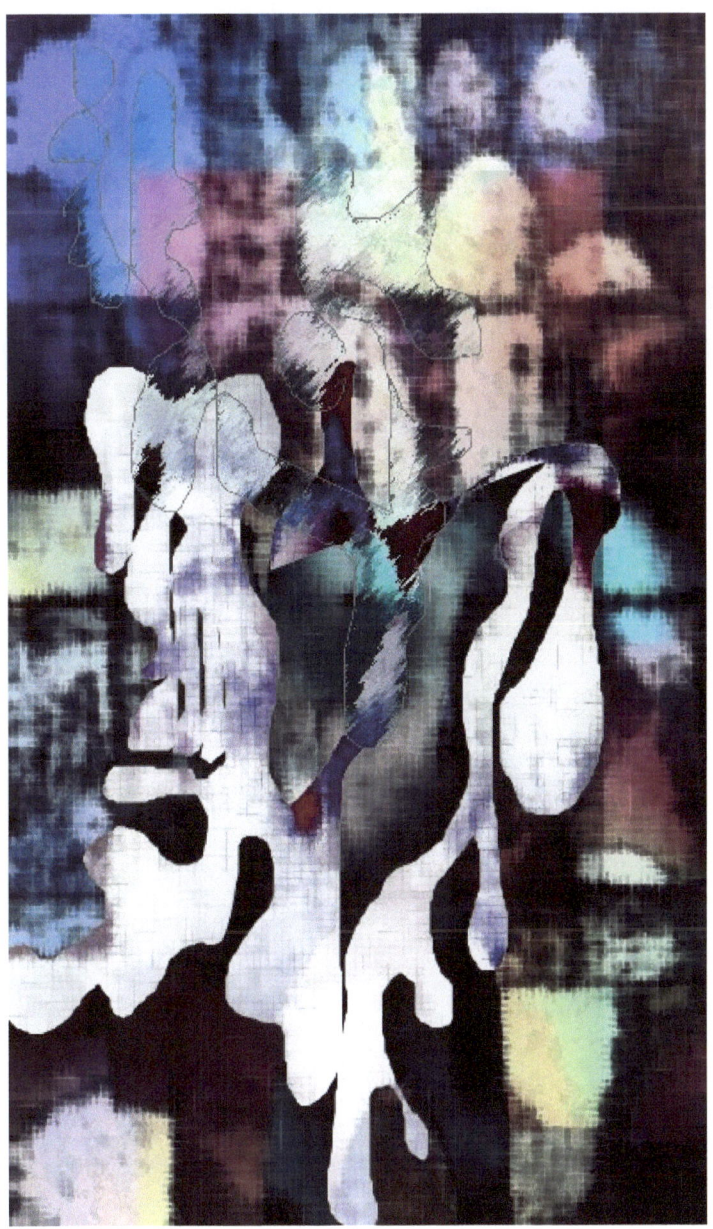

Untitled

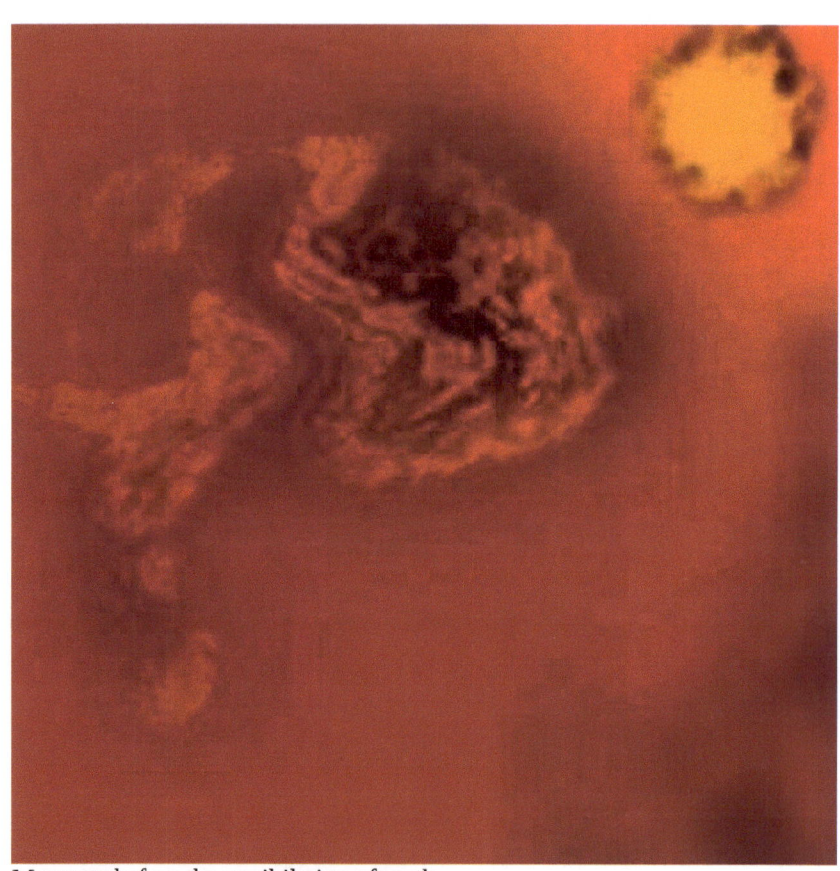

Moments before the annihilation of earth

Hope and despair

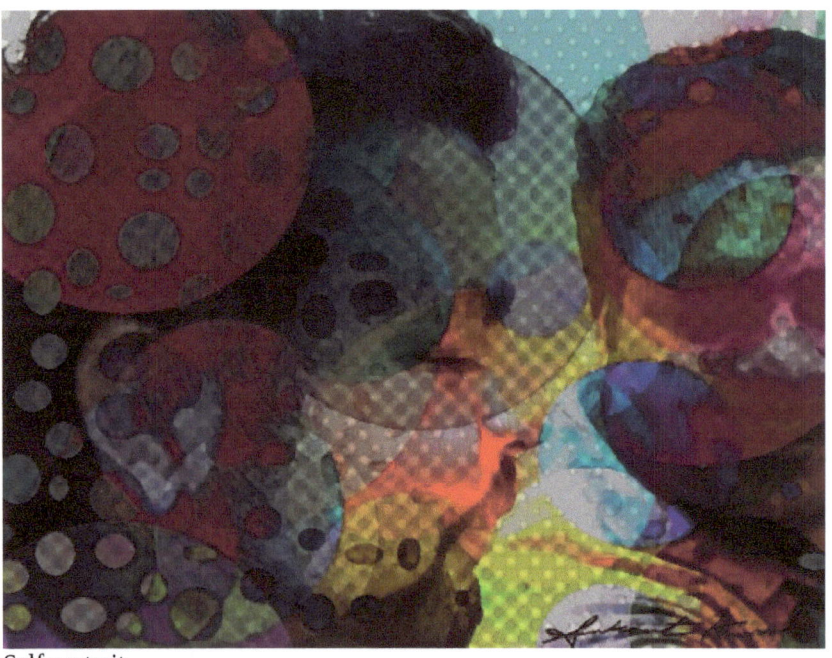
Self portrait

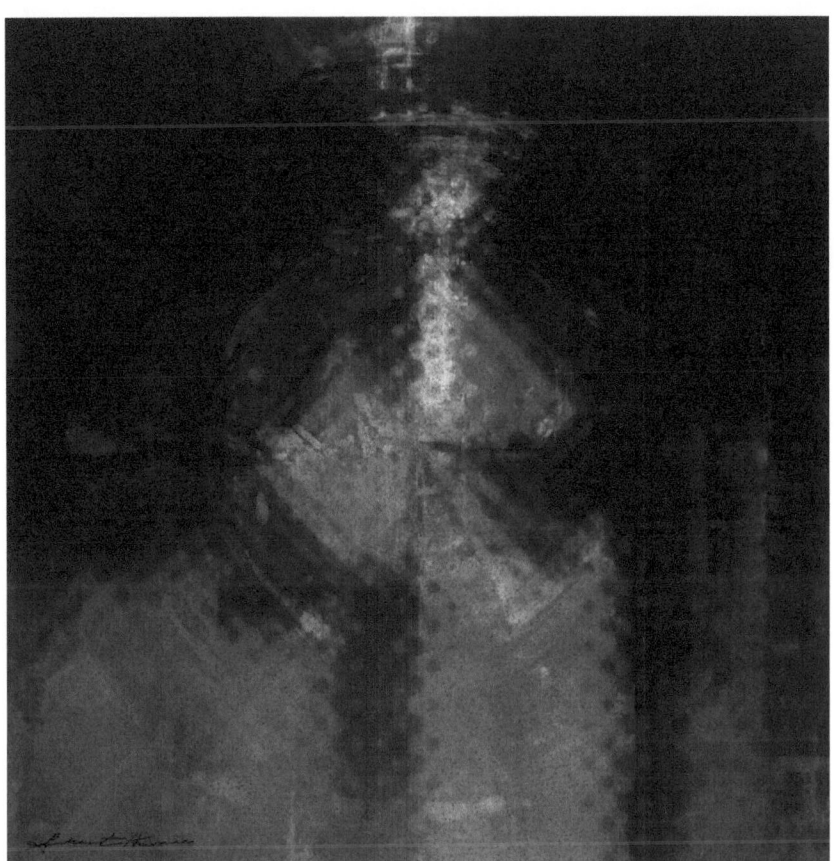

Light through cracks

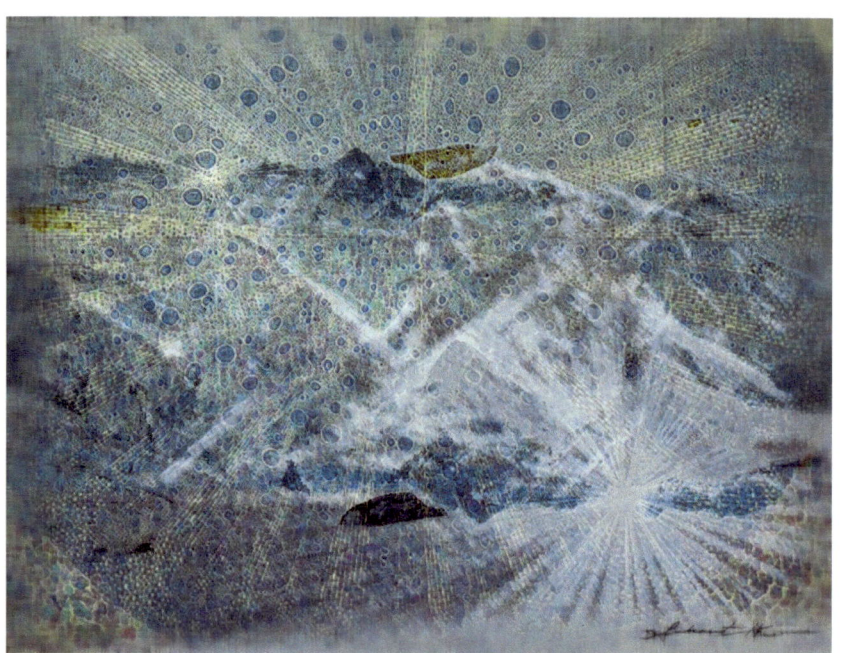

Diatomicius rain

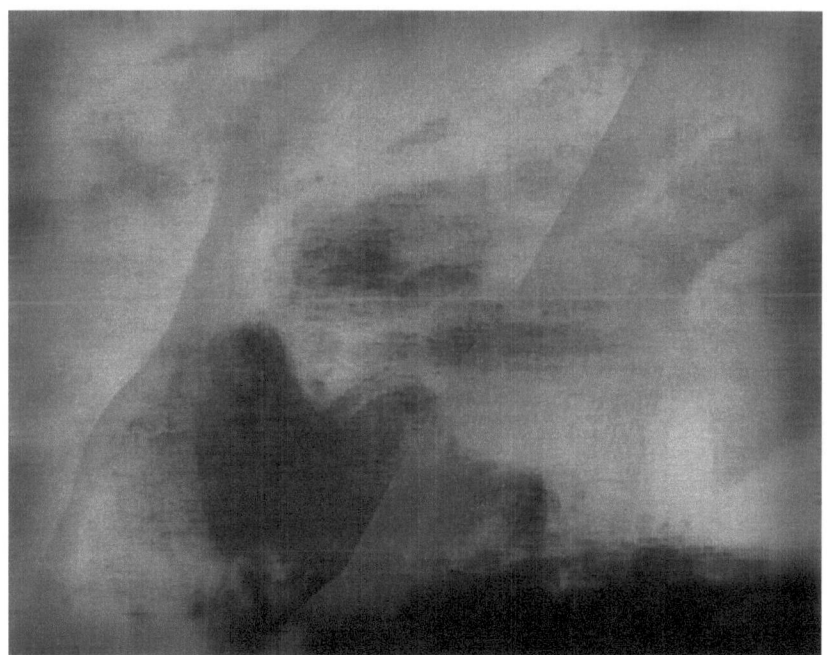

Winds on the winding roads

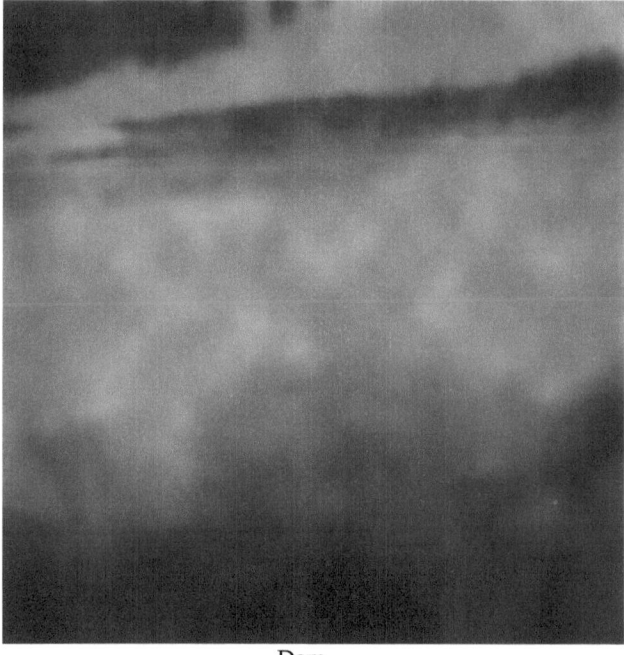

Dam

Dreams from down under

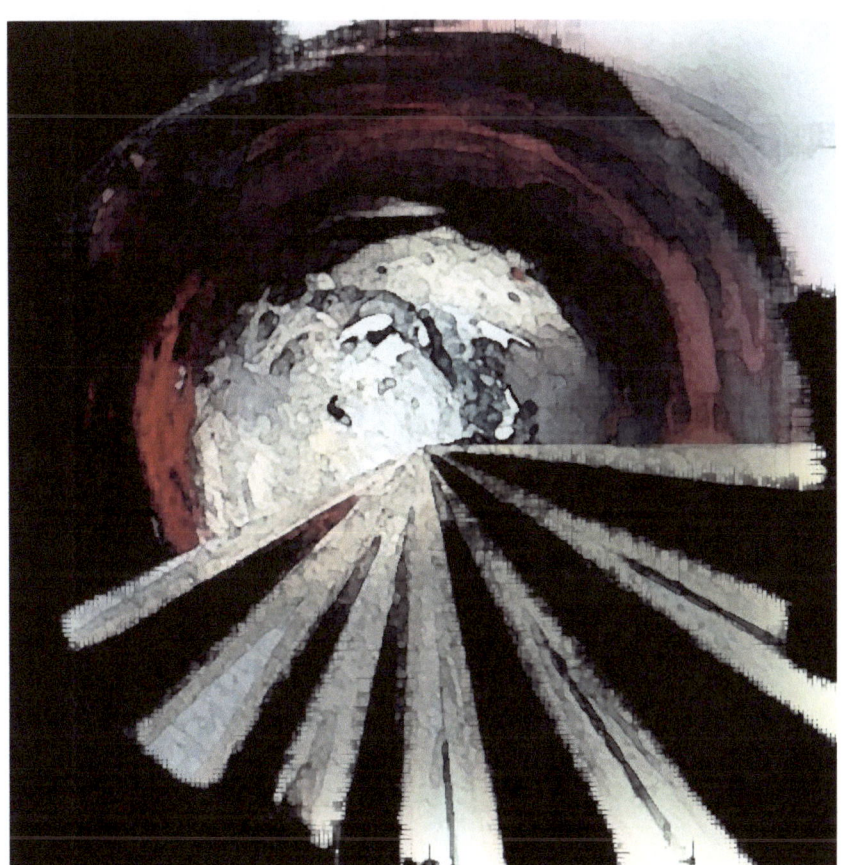

Indian spring?

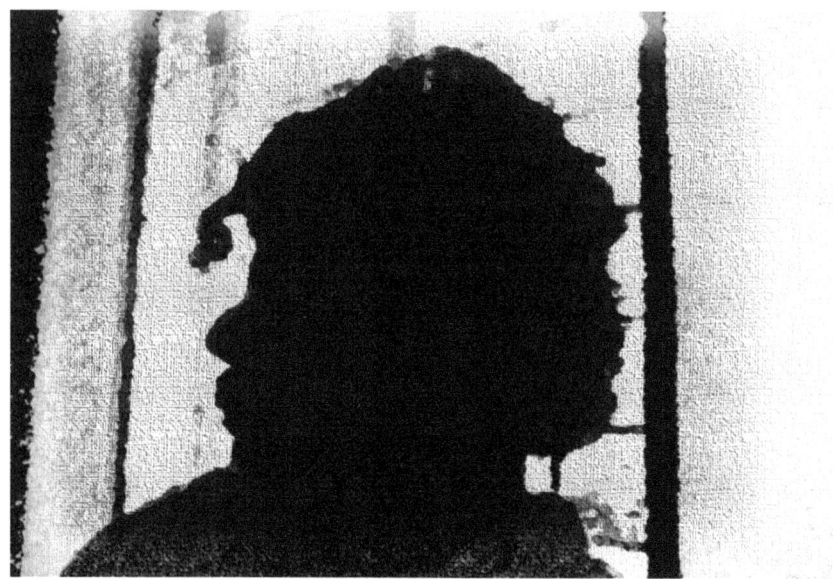

Self portrait in dark times of Bengal stay

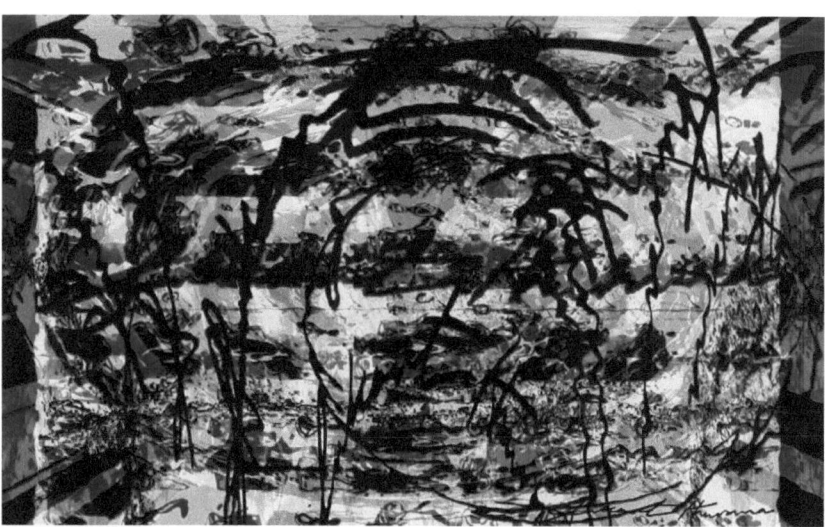

"Humility": Juxtaposition and distortion of my signatures (sarcasm intended in the title).

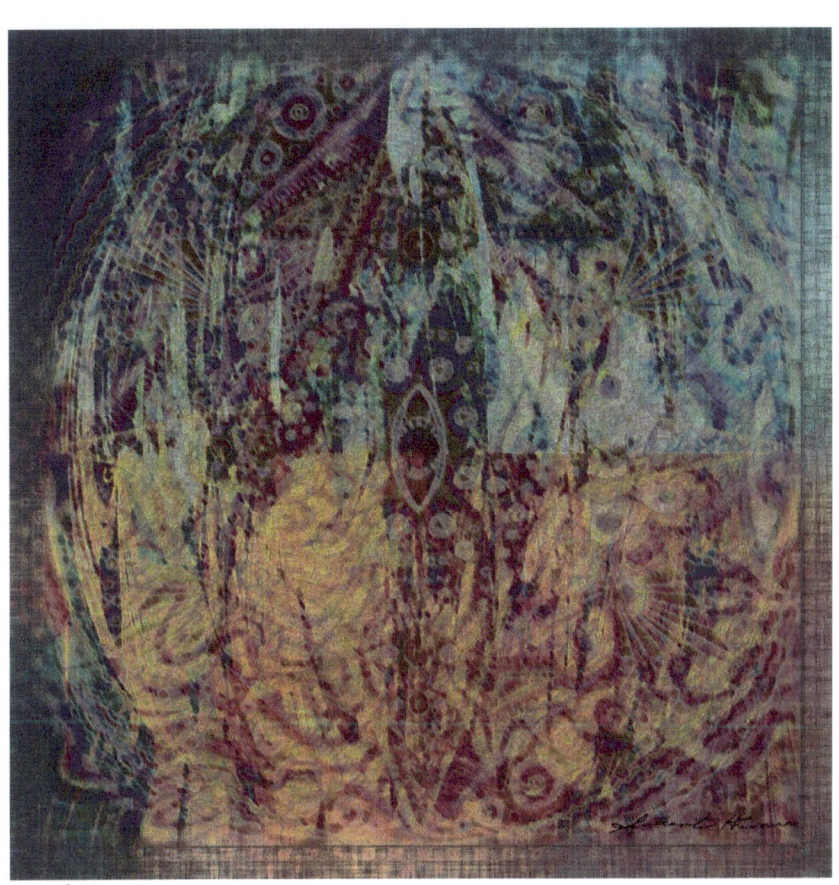

Fourth Eye

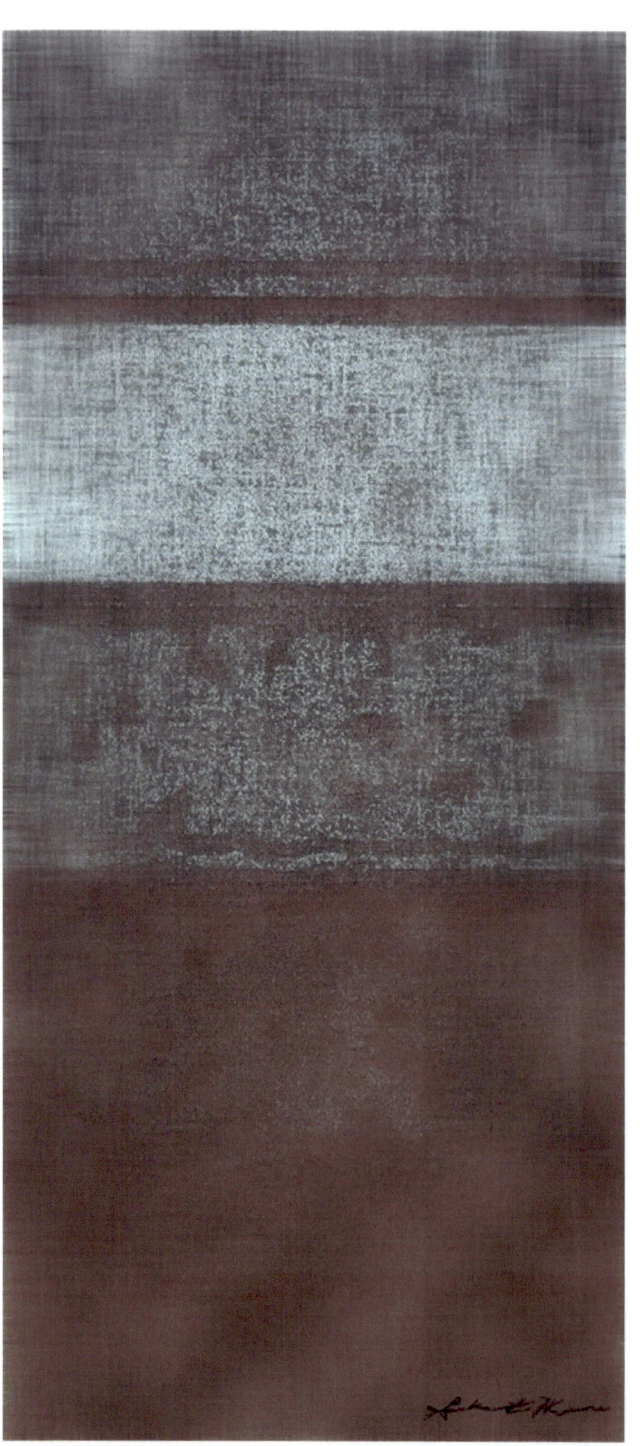

After few
conversations

Not my circus anymore

Note: I have penned works and held autobiographical art exhibitions that explore my love of New World and free thinking and how I eventually cut off my emotional umbilical chord with some of the ways of Old World but for ages I not just worked and wrote for a liberal and more tolerant South Asia but also made several art works to that end. Here are two examples of digital studies that I did to eventually make acrylic works on Canvas. Embrace of one world over another was not simply because of few devastating web attacks at a crucial stage of my carrier, a physical threat on life that fortunately due to being a popular teacher was saved by students jumping in the situation, financial attacks, but eventually realizing my weakness in inability to change much in the Old World and stupidly losing years that could have smartly been used to in my limited ways to improve all of the world through science, technology, and art. While I was stupid and foolhardy... and I hope that I have learned enough for remaining life from my past mistakes but here is a brief visual example of past activism.

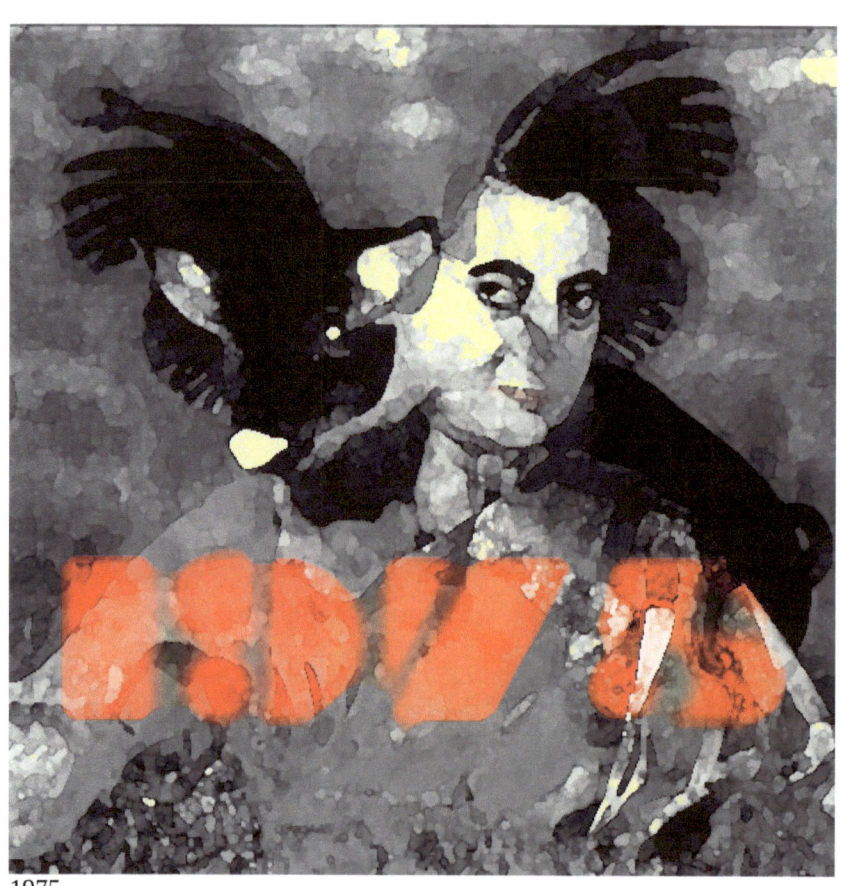

1975

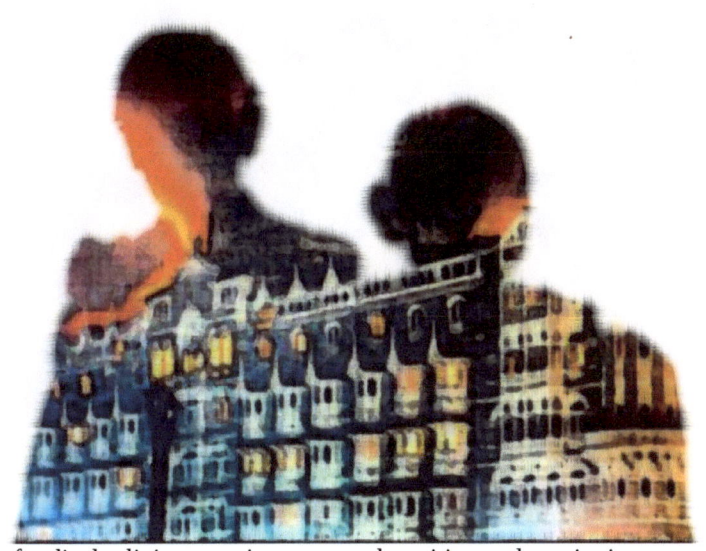

Dangers of radical religious sentiments: a sad partition and continuing tremors. (Two of the several founding fathers of modern South Asian countries, Gandhi and Jinnah in form of the burning hotel Taj, an aftermath of terrorist attack on Mumbai)

Celebrating colors and forms

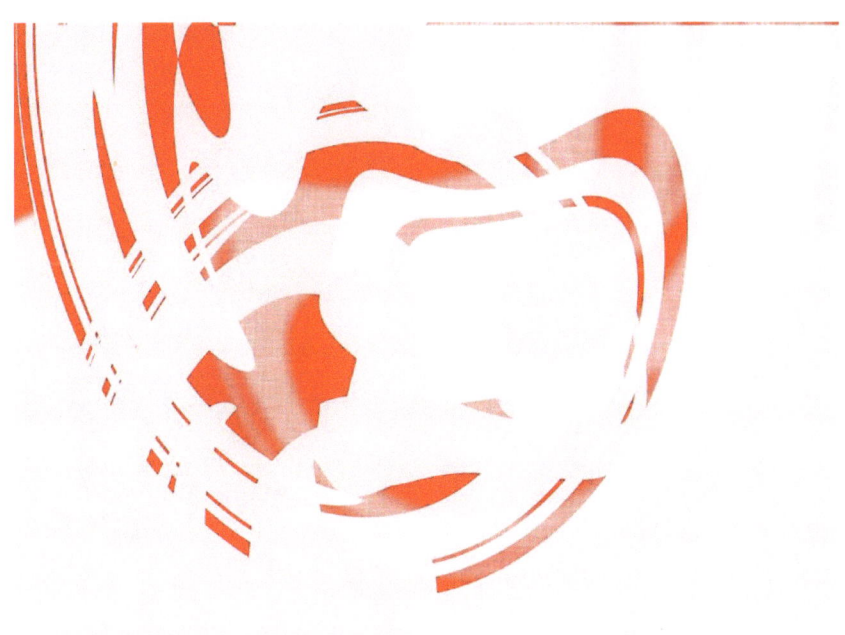

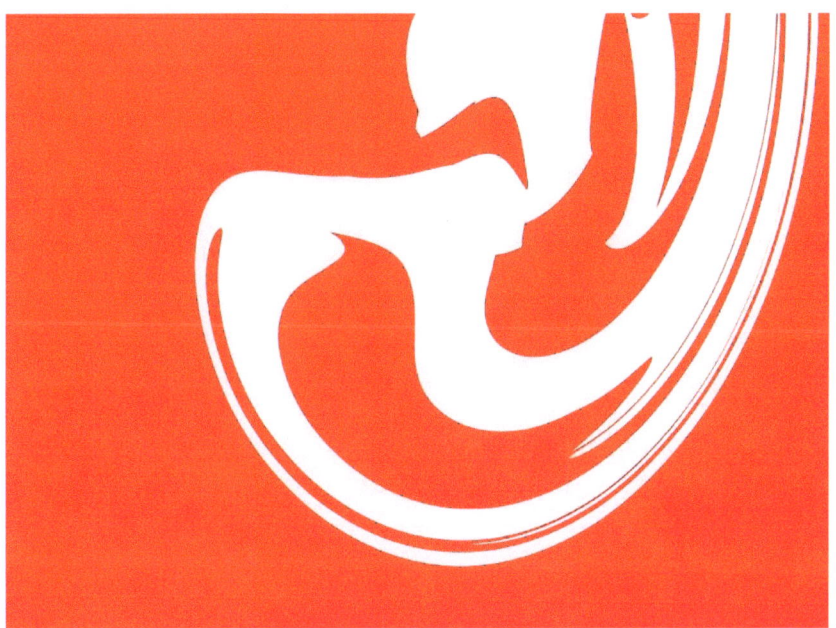

Untitled bi-chromatics

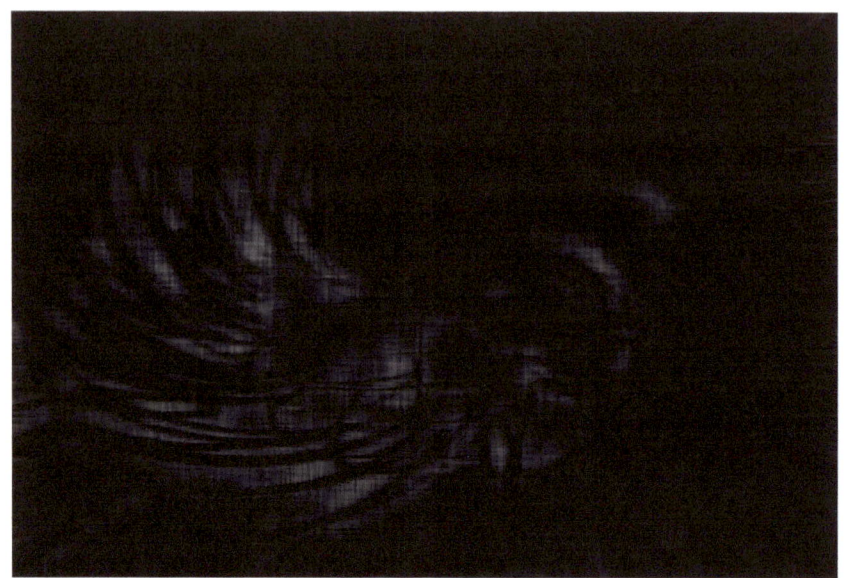

Only dark, not deep, an exercise in un-art

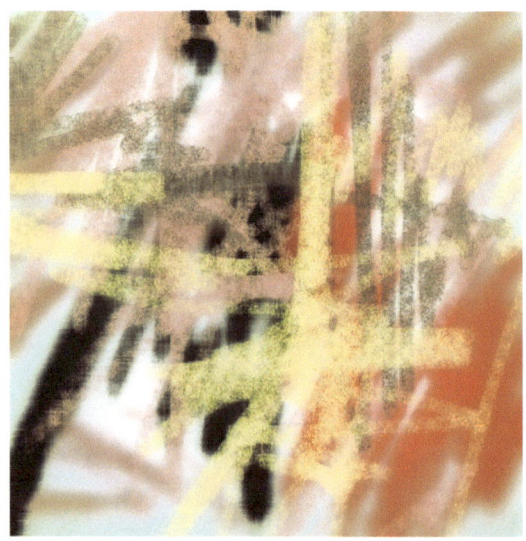

Neither dark nor deep and not completely fine with it; an exercise in un-art

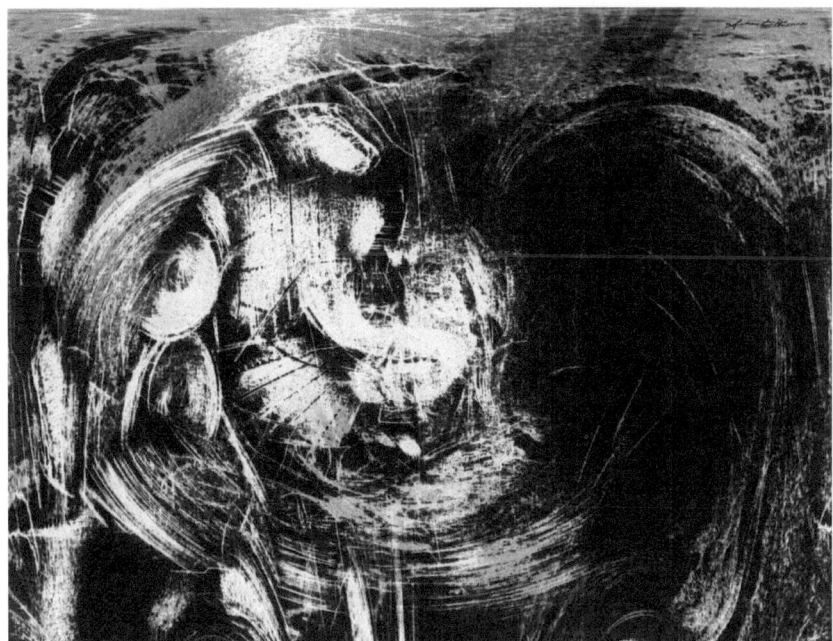

Where did I forget my black palette. Last I saw it was next to chillies, next to onions.

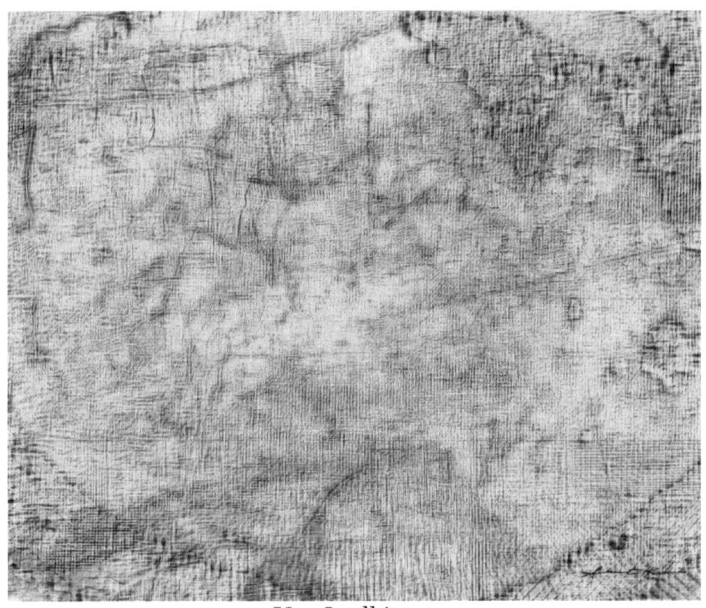

Yes, I call it art

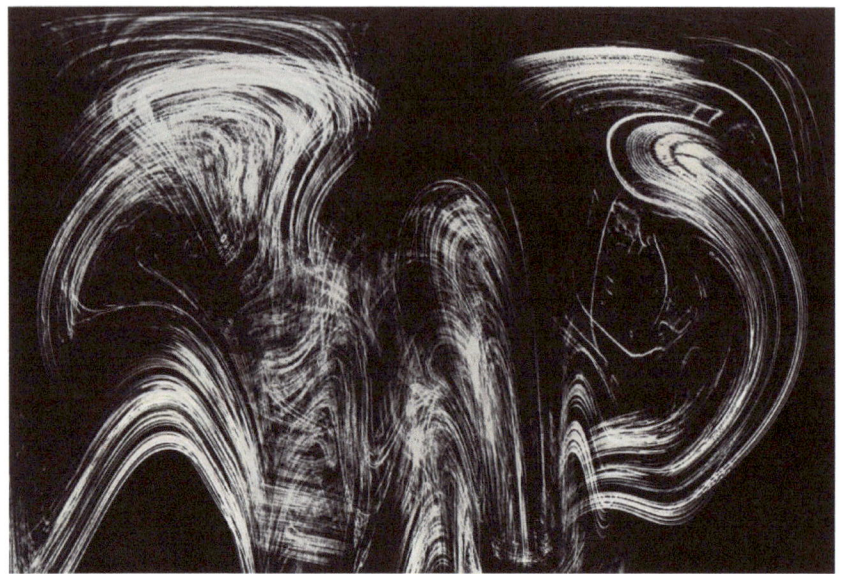

Antigravity

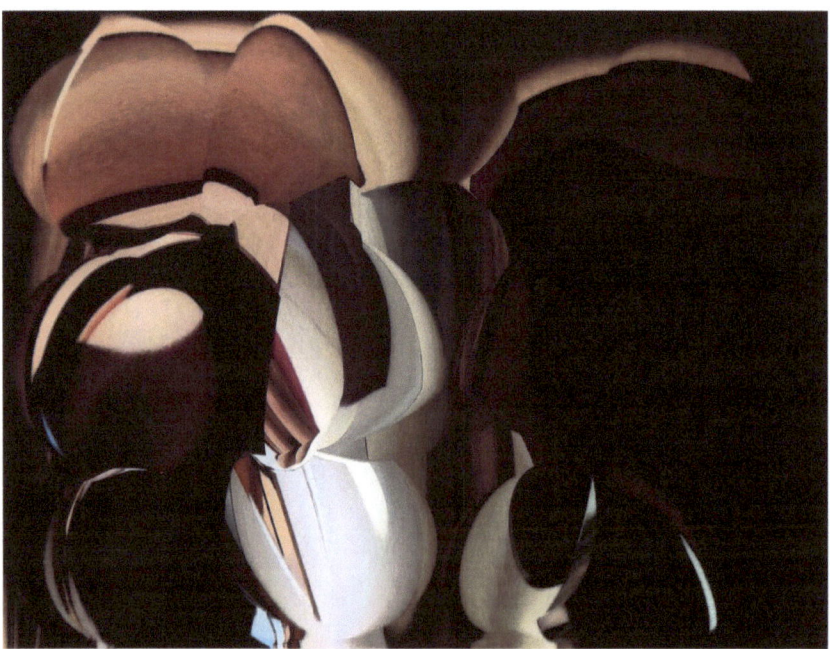

In search of a story to account for this random walk

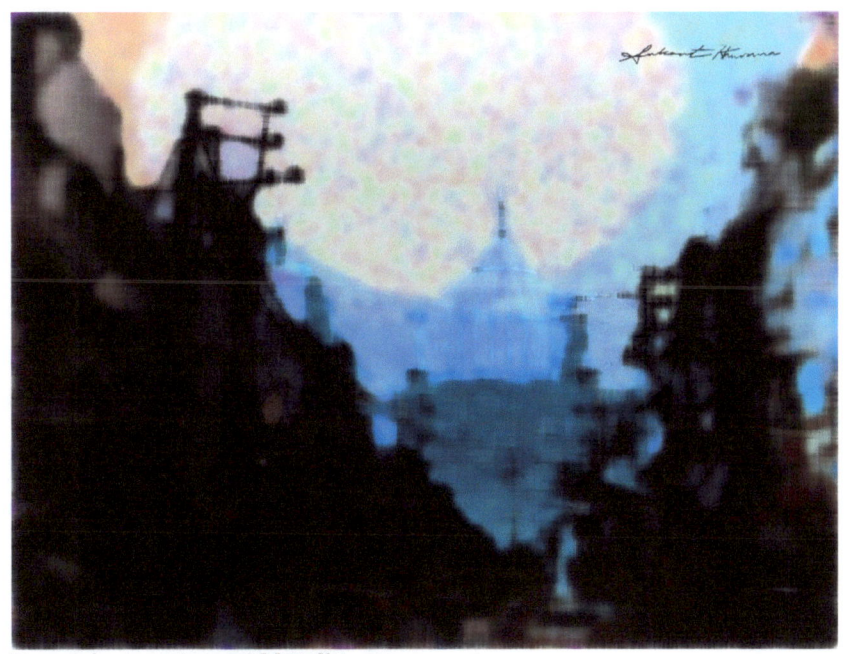

Remembering trips to Old Delhi.

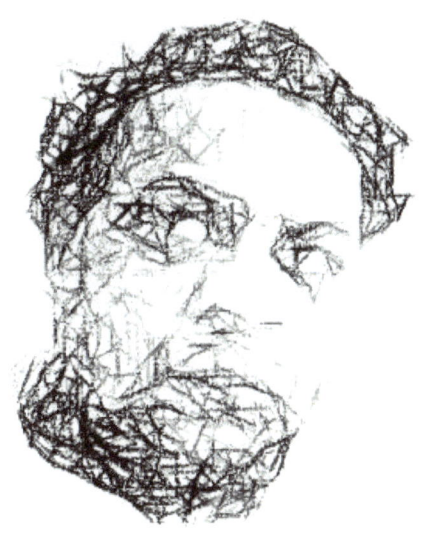

Temporary silence

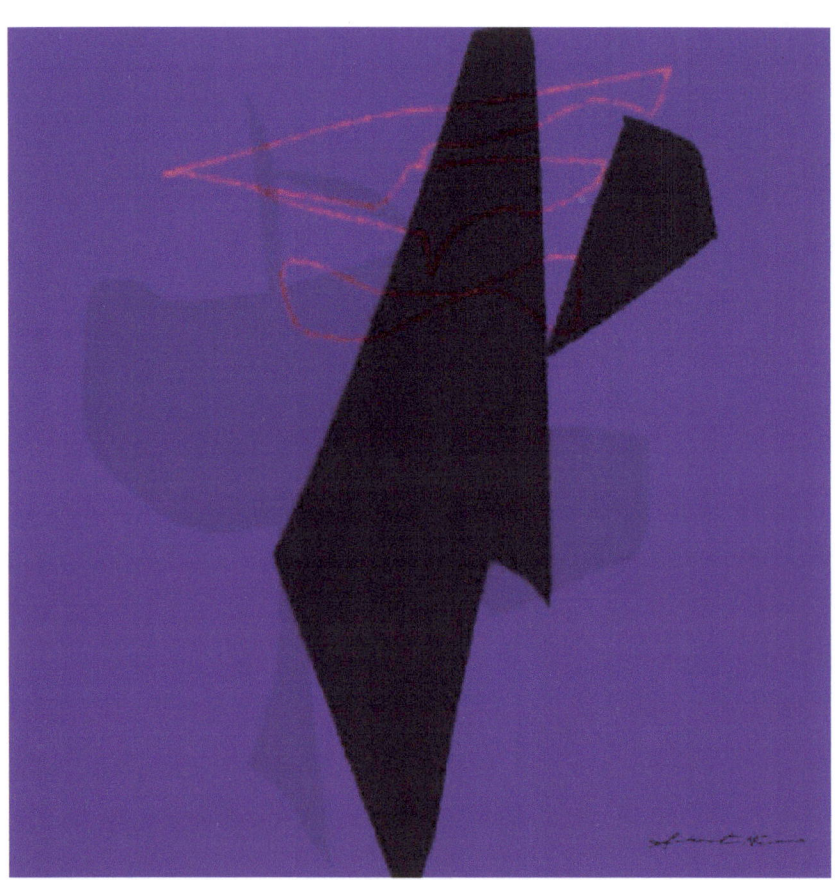

Homage to Prince

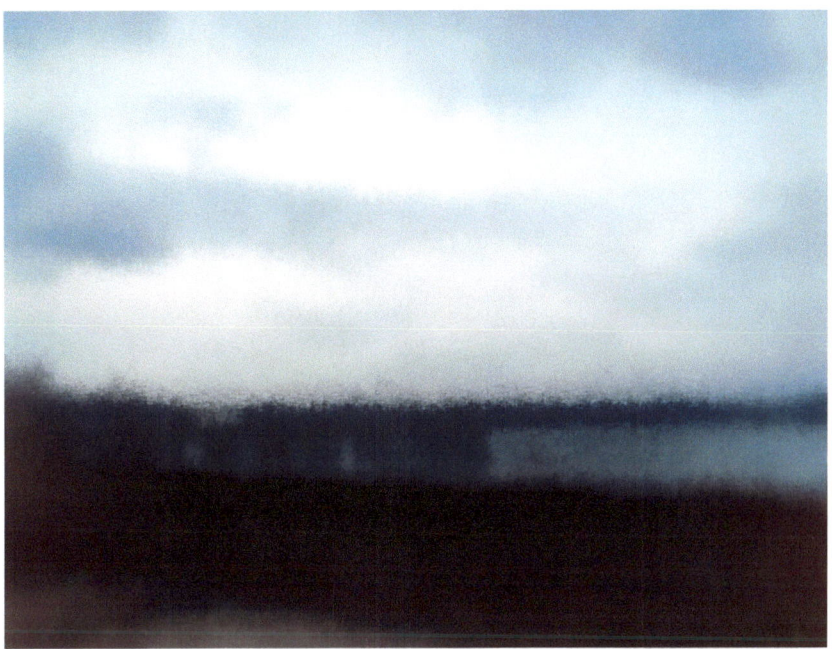

Inner harbor

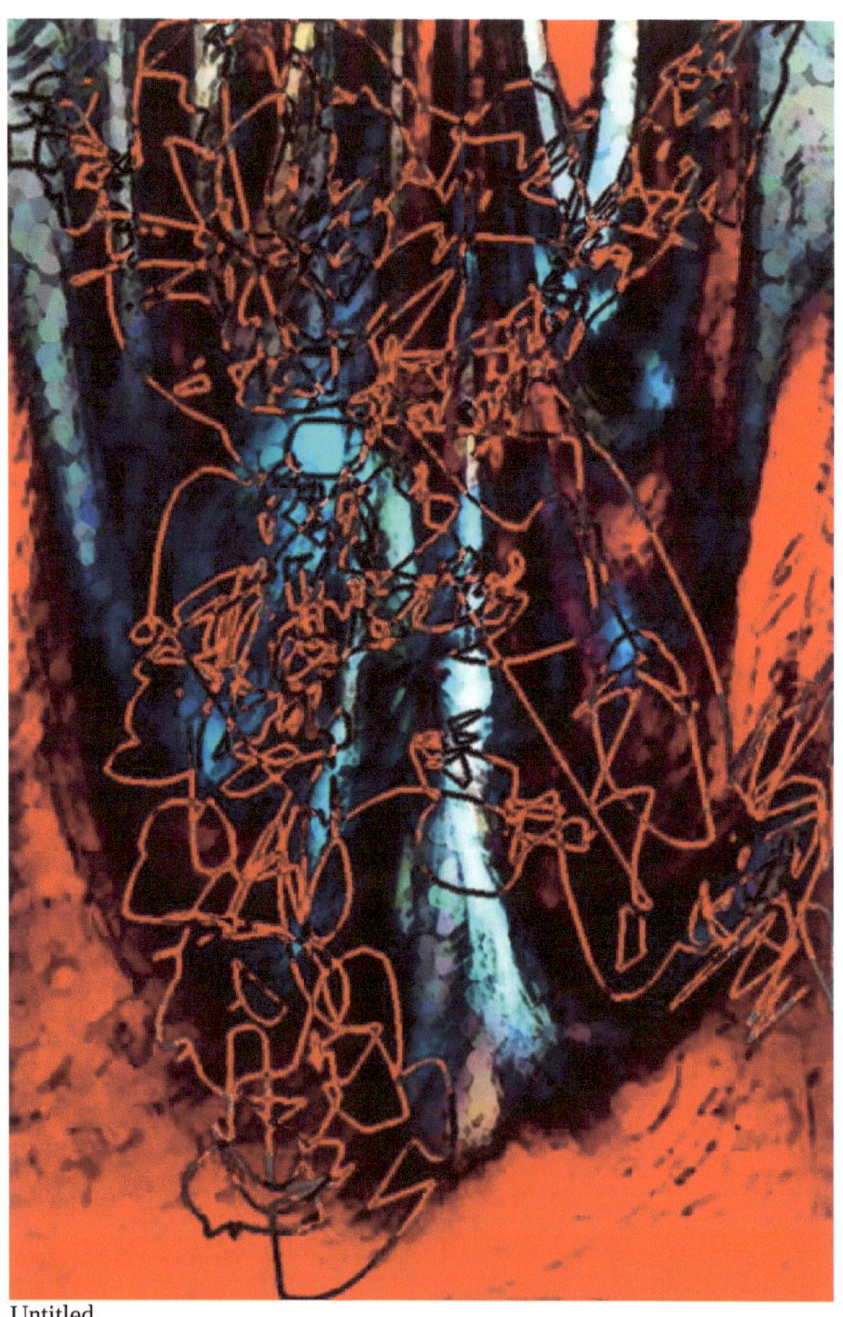

Untitled

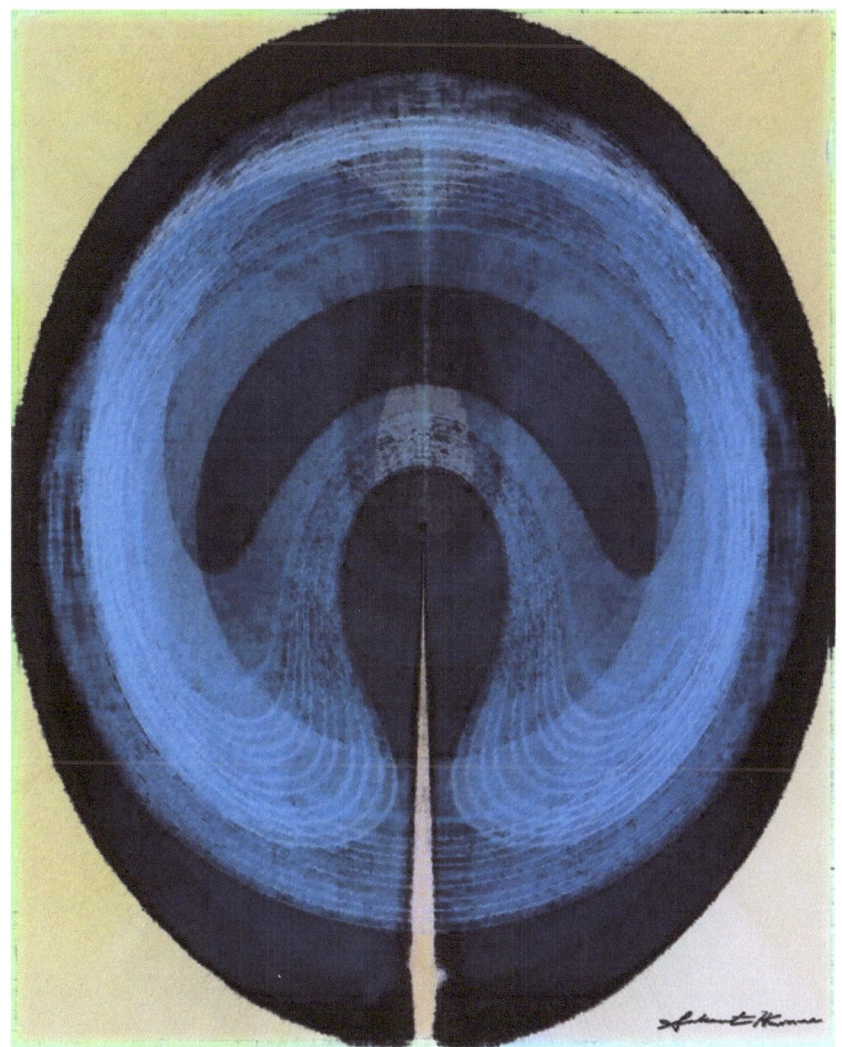

A new beginning

www.ingramcontent.com/pod-product-compliance
Lightning Source LLC
Chambersburg PA
CBHW040814200526
45159CB00024B/2961